The Banks of Canada in the Commonwealth Caribbean

The Banks of Canada in the Commonwealth Caribbean
Economic Nationalism and Multinational Enterprises of a Medium Power

Daniel Jay Baum

AN AUTHORS GUILD BACKINPRINT.COM EDITION

The Banks of Canada
in the Commonwealth Caribbean
Economic Nationalism and Multinational Enterprises of a Medium Power

AN AUTHORS GUILD BACKINPRINT.COM EDITION

Published by iUniverse, Inc.

For information address:
iUniverse, Inc.
2021 Pine Lake Road, Suite 100
Lincoln, NE 68512
www.iuniverse.com

Originally published by Praeger Publishers

Because of the dynamic nature of the Internet, any Web addresses
or links contained in this book may have changed
since publication and may no longer be valid.

The views expressed in this work are solely those of the author and do not necessarily reflect
the views of the publisher, and the publisher hereby disclaims any responsibility for them.

ISBN: 978-0-595-47603-9

Printed in the United States of America

Many persons assisted in this study, covering a period of two years. Government officials at the highest levels both in Canada and in the Commonwealth Caribbean gave freely of their time. I received generous cooperation from the Canadian banking community and also from English and American bankers in the Commonwealth Caribbean. Space limitations and a promise not to disclose the names of some individuals prevents me from thanking the many persons who helped me, although at various points in the study specific names do appear.

I should like to express my very deep appreciation to Ms. Karen Orloff Kaplan, M.S.W., for her help with the personal aspects of nationalism and to my colleague Professor Norman May for his assistance with Chapter 3, "The Laws Regulating Canadian Banks in the Caribbean." In addition, I thank my colleagues Professors Francis Snyder and Johann Mohr for their comments touching upon the anthropological and personality aspects of the subject.

The project itself was made possible by a grant from the Canada Council. The typing and retyping of drafts was done patiently and well by my administrative assistant, Ms. April Seal. Finally, I thank my wife, Harriet, for reading the manuscript in its various drafts and offering incisive comment.

CONTENTS

The Banks of Canada in the Commonwealth Caribbean

There is in the world today a tide of nationalism, a quest for self-identification, and an attack against the global or multinational corporation, which is seen as an impediment to self-determination. The purpose of this book is to probe the rationality of the attack and question the goals of the attackers. Much of the substantive portion of the study will focus on the oldest and most powerful of the global corporations, the banks. Of all the entities capable of avoiding the rigors of "good corporate citizenship," the banks stand first. They, after all, whether operating as commercial or merchant bankers, can limit their direct investment in any host country. Money, unlike an oil well, is fungible, notwithstanding foreign exchange controls.

The Canadian banks were selected for study for several reasons. (1) Of the capitalist nations Canada probably is least identified as an imperialistic power. (2) The Canadian banks are subject to tight central control by the federal government; they can properly be viewed as a mechanism for the achievement of national policy. (3) The power of the Canadian banks is patent: Five Canadian banks control 90 percent of banking assets. The banks, in turn, hold 40 percent of all financial institution assets, and the five largest banks stand among the world's largest banks operating on a global scene. (4) As a nation, and as an affluent nation, Canada has evidenced the same concern for nationalism and self-identification that so often tends to be imputed only to developing nations. (5) By examining the role of Canadian banks abroad—as global corporations—a better measure might be taken of the meaning and the reality of so-called good corporate citizenship.

There exists a specific area of the world where the larger Canadian banks have long done business and where they have long been in a dominant position not only in relation to other banks but even in relation to governments. That area is what some call the

Commonwealth Caribbean. Loosely, it stretches from Bermuda to Trinidad and Tobago and Guyana, covering a distance of more than 1,200 miles. It consists of not one but numerous nation-states which on more than one occasion, despite ties to the Crown, have rejected regionalism. Yet its population is limited; there are only about 4 million people living in what will be the ambit of this study: Bahamas, Jamaica, the "Associated States," Barbados, and Trinidad and Tobago.

Each of these nation-states has recently achieved independence over at least its internal affairs. Each is what must be called a developing nation. Each is seeking its own way toward economic independence, self-determination, and the power to shape self-identification. In each island-nation individually and collectively the Canadian banks are powerful, if not dominant. Our concern will be to discover how the Canadian banks function, how they view their position, and how they are viewed by the Caribbean governments and population.

CANADA AS A WORLD POWER

Canada is a wealthy nation. Indeed, among the nations of the world Canada's position is unique. By the year 2000 only Canada and three other nations—the United States, Japan, and Sweden—will move from an advanced industrial society to one that might be called post-industrial. The differences between levels of economic society in terms of per capita yearly income will be significant. The post-industrial society's per capita income will be between $4,000 and $20,000. This contrasts with the advanced industrial society's per capita income of $1,500-$4,000; the industrial society's per capita income of $600-$1,500; the partly industrialized society's per capita income of $200-$600, and the preindustrial society's per capita income of $50-$200.[1]

Difference in income, however, will be but one of the characteristics of the postindustrial society. By the year 2000 Canadian economic activity will have shifted somewhat from agriculture and industrial production, the first and second areas, to service and research, the third and fourth areas. By itself neither private enterprise nor the marketplace will be the determinants of just how the economic activity of the "cerebral" revolution takes shape.[2]

The scenario for the year 2000 is not too difficult for Canada to visualize, for some glimpses already have been seen. In contrast to the United States, Canada has long seen itself as a hewer of wood and drawer of water. It is rich as an agricultural and mining nation, and by 1972 it found that such a position was not without its rewards. In that year, a worldwide need for its wheat and natural resources became apparent. Both the Soviet Union and Communist China asked for large quantities of Canadian wheat, and both Japan and the United States had become willing buyers of Canadian fuel whether it be electricity, gas, or coal. Japan purchased more than a $1 billion (U.S.) supply of coal from British Columbia in 1972, and the United States began to fund a $1 billion (U.S.) electricity project in Quebec.

Neither Canadian wheat nor fuel sales were entered into as purely private projects. Both the federal and provincial governments stood as principals. In many instances the federal government initiated the projects, and in all instances it approved them.

Canada's greatest treasure trove, however, may well prove to be the great northern expanse reaching into the Arctic, land that the federal government alone controls. Enormous natural resources have been found there, chief among which is oil. The government has clearly demonstrated a willingness to exercise dominion over the land and to see it fully exploited.

Oil rigs now dot the Arctic landscape. Major north-south and east-west highways are under construction, and pipelines are scheduled to be laid alongside the highways. The federal government has imparted a sense of urgency to the building. Both domestic and foreign enterprises, all under government license, are engaged in extensive exploration. To tie the ribbon of highway with other forms of communication and transportation, Canada in 1972 launched its first domestic satellite, specifically designed to bring instant communication to the north. And, in 1972, Canada began negotiations with West German firms with a view toward the construction of tankers able to pass through Arctic waters.

Canada as a nation seems bent on exploiting its own resources, processing and refining them, and, if possible, placing itself in the most favorable position to deliver the final products. The way was paved for this in 1970 when Canada attempted jurisdictional control of Arctic waters for an area extending to 100 miles from shore. The justification offered by the Canadian government was the need to protect the ecology of the Arctic; the tundra was highly sensitive to change.[3] In point of fact, if it is successful in its claim, Canada will have succeeded in stopping U.S. shipments of oil from Alaska to the American east coast. In addition, it will have inhibited the incentive for American initiatives in developing new northern tankers such as the Manhattan. Without impugning Canadian motives, the fact remains that Canada as a government made practical, hard decisions designed to place the nation as such in the best possible position to exploit its own resources.

Neither the tension of confederation nor a history firmly rooted in free enterprise has ever stopped the Canadian government from engaging in expansive economic enterprises. And whatever were the rigors and challenges of constructing the transcontinental railroad, they are in a very real sense dwarfed by the emerging development of the Canadian north.

Wealth will flow to Canada and Canadians from this northern development. How will that wealth be used? In asking the question and positing some answers, the reality of Canada's position by the year 2000 tends to come into sharper focus. The wealth will go to the government and to its citizens. The government is likely to use a portion of it to fund or support the development of Canadian global corporations. All of the nation's major parties seem committed to such a position, and the 1972 Federal Report on Foreign Direct Investment—The Gray Report—offers the rationale: The global corporation is dominating much of the world's economy. For our purpose, the global corporation is defined as embodying direct foreign investment by a single enterprise in at least four or five nation-states, dividing its activities among them with a view toward realizing overall corporate profits.[4]

The Gray Report estimated the world gross national product (GNP) at $3,000 billion, of which $2,350 billion is produced in the noncommunist world.* Of this noncommunist portion of world GNP, about $450 billion, or 19 percent, is accounted for by foreign-controlled subsidiaries. The figure rises sharply when the United States GNP is discounted: out of $1,350 billion of GNP in the noncommunist world outside the U.S., $350 billion, or 26 percent, is accounted for by foreign subsidiaries.[5]

The majority of the world's global corporations are American controlled. What they produce and sell far exceeds direct American exports. The Gray Report estimates that American global corporations through their subsidiaries produce about $200 billion (U.S.) in goods annually while American exports amount to only $30 billion (U.S.) annually.[6] Yet it is not only U.S. corporations that have been expanding their international business:

> One study of the 500 largest industrial corporations in the world (approximately 300 United States and 200 non-United States) shows that in the 10 years following the formation of the Common Market (1957-67), United States Corporations have not been outstripping their rivals. Rather, they fell behind from 1957-62 and only managed to keep pace between 1962 and 1967. This reflects, in part, the deliberate strategy of European and Japanese governments of

---

*Denominations in the Gray Report are given in the British system, in which 1,000 million equals the American billion and 1,000 billion equals the American trillion.

fostering MNEs [multinational enterprises] rooted in their jurisdiction.[7]

The global corporation, or MNE, is a primary instrument for development, for maximizing domestic growth potential. By capturing overseas markets it returns revenue to the home country for research and technological improvements that can restart the cycle by stimulating even deeper foreign penetration.[8] At the same time, expansion beyond domestic boundaries allows an expanded outlet for the nation's talent. Not without reason does the Mining Association of Canada advise Canadians: "Wherever there is exploration for resources in this world you are likely to find a Canadian. We have developed a technology that others need."[9]

CANADA'S BANKS AS MULTINATIONAL ENTERPRISES

If the past is prologue, it should be clear that Canada will develop global enterprises wherever possible. It already has done so in an area most important to any national economy. I refer specifically to what an early federal report on foreign ownership called the "commanding heights" of the economy, namely, finance. With purpose, Canada through its federal government caused financial control to reside in the banking industry, which is subject to exclusive federal jurisdiction. Indeed, a bank's charter is the Bank Act. The federal government rather severely limits the numbers of those that might wish to become banks. There are limits on foreign share ownership (no more than 10 percent), there is the capacity for direct intervention by the Governor of the Bank of Canada, and indeed there is regular consultation between the Governor and banking management.

The five largest Canadian banks are world banks; they meet the primary tests of the Gray Report as global corporations. They have taken some of their own moneys—that is, company funds—and established either branch or subsidiary operations in four or five non-Canadian economies; but, as with all efficient world enterprises, they have had to use only a minimal amount of their own funds. They have often been able to rely on the deposits of the countries where they are located to conduct their business of making loans. On the whole, as Chapter 4 makes plain, there has been no interference by Canadian governmental authorities with the conduct of the world activities of Canadian banks.

In the area of the Commonwealth Caribbean, Canadian banks are dominant and, in fact, control finance. On some of the islands a single Canadian bank might dominate; it might control the flow and direction of available savings. The status of Canadian banks, though unpublicized in Canada, is well known in the Commonwealth Caribbean. It is not a status newly created—Canadian banks have been established in the area for more than half a century.

In this setting it is appropriate to quote from the Gray Report:

> If MNEs were to develop to the point where they become
> the major organizers of production in the world, they
> would undoubtedly wield substantially more power than
> they do already. But power responsible to whom? At the
> moment power is wielded largely by national govern-
> ments responsible to their electorates. In a world dom-
> inated by large and powerful MNEs, to whom would non-
> elected boards and management of multinational enter-
> prises be responsible? Domestic corporations are
> generally subject to national control, but there is, as yet,
> no international legal order which could control MNEs.[10]

THE COMMONWEALTH CARIBBEAN: AN AREA OF CANADIAN FINANCIAL DOMINATION

In our study of the role of Canadian banks in the Commonwealth Caribbean, it is well to bear in mind the Gray Report's question: To whom are nonelected boards and managements of multinational enter- prises responsible? The question becomes all the more pointed for our subject is not the American global corporation but the Canadian global corporation. Moreover, the nation-states where the Canadian MNEs operate are relatively weak; they are developing nations with per capita incomes ranging from $500 to $1,500 annually. Yet they are in an area of the world proximate to North America and they share part of a common cultural base with Canada—the English language, and English rule. They are in contact with the affluence of North America, but despite their independence they themselves do not share in that affluence. For a number of reasons, both rational and irrational, there is a Commonwealth Caribbean sense of being exploited, and an answer is found for many in what must be described as black nation- alism. Not infrequently, Canadian banks as holders of money find themselves the object of blame. After all, so the argument might run, the banks hold the money; if the banks used their deposits in the interests of the people, then the people would prosper. To Canadians, the argument might appear naïve and irrational. Yet, let it be re- membered that nationalism, even Canadian nationalism, is not always rational in its expression. Moreover, the problem of Commonwealth Caribbean response becomes more understandable if one views this rather crude social model: On any one island about half the population is under fifteen. Unemployment is high and educational opportunities low. There is a large but diminishing peasant class of small farmers (20-40 percent of the population) who work hard but earn less than any other employable group. Their crops are few, such as sugar and bananas, and more likely than not the world price is depressed. There is a steady drift to already overcrowded cities. Employment is sought preferably in the few existing industries such as oil refining or bauxite mining, where pay is relatively high. But available positions are fully taken, and no more than 10 to 15 percent of the population hold jobs in these few industries.

For the rest of the population there is employment in the service sector. This usually means tourist-related industries. The jobs range from busboys to waiters, hotel clerks, and taxi drivers. Until the 1970s expatriates, often English or Canadian, served as hotel managers, chefs, and even lifeguards. Black nationalism with its attendant work-permit restrictions is changing this, and for the first time Caribbean nationals are moving into managerial positions.

Still, no more than 5 to 10 percent of the population could be called middle class. They are the newly named managerial group and the emerging native civil service. They live in the homes formerly occupied by English shopkeepers and managers. And often it is for them that government initiates housing projects.

Color remains a dominant fact of Commonwealth Caribbean life. On the whole, the natives are black and the tourists are white. Where native color moves from black to brown, then brown tends to be favored. Where there is a significant Asian or East Indian minority that has prospered, then that minority can, like the whites, be a target of criticism by black nationalists.

The intellectual leadership of the nation-state is not in the university; it is not in the academic community. The university as a source of intellectual leadership is removed from the mainstream of the community, and such intellectual leadership as exists comes from a few, a very few, highly talented civil servants and from political leaders. The politicians and civil servants for the most part tend to be practical rather than intellectual.   Indeed, this is made necessary in part by the trade union movement, which is action-oriented and heavily involved in politics.

Despite the pressures of black nationalism, there remains a small but influential expatriate community which owns the banks, hotels, oil refineries, and bauxite mines. As individual representatives of world businesses, the expatriates are talented and able to call upon the resources of their organizations to serve the best interests of the island government—but they do not. They prefer to keep a "low profile." Alongside the expatriate community must be placed their home governments, who stand not only as substantial trading partners but also as providers of major foreign aid grants. In the Commonwealth Caribbean, for example, the Canadian annual contribution to the four million inhabitants is $5 per person. On some of the islands the figure is as high as $16 per person.

This is the setting in which the Canadian world banks operate. Our concern is with how they enact their role, how they are received by the Commonwealth Caribbean, and how the Canadian government might meld national business interests with the needs of less powerful developing countries. Out of such a melding might come a more sophisticated response to nationalism and the global corporation.

NOTES

1. See D. J. Baum, "The Global Corporation: An American Challenge to the Nation-State?," Iowa Law Review, 55 (1969): 412.

2. Ibid.

3. See J. Saywell, ed., Canadian Annual Review for 1970 (Toronto: University of Toronto Press), pp. 349-53.

4. Foreign Direct Investment in Canada (Ottawa: Information Canada, 1972). Hereinafter cited as the Gray Report.

5. Ibid., pp. 52-53.

6. Ibid., p. 53.

7. Ibid., pp. 53-54.

8. Ibid., pp. 56-57.

9. Ibid., p. 61.

10. Ibid., p. 61.

2

THE GROWTH OF CANADIAN BANKING IN THE COMMONWEALTH CARIBBEAN

THE IMPORTANCE OF THE COMMONWEALTH CARIBBEAN TO CANADIAN BANKING

The largest of Canadian banks are world enterprises. They have offices in London, Dublin, Paris, Athens, and in the developing Third World ranging from Africa to Latin America and the West Indies. They have not newly come to their status as global enterprises. As early as 1855 the first agency of a Canadian bank was established in New York City. Before the turn of the century, in 1889, the Bank of Nova Scotia opened a branch office in Kingston, Jamaica.

The growth of Canadian banks operating outside Canada both in branches and assets has been steady and, more recently, even spectacular. Forrest L. Rogers, Economic Adviser to the Bank of Nova Scotia, noted in 1971 the long-established ties between the larger Canadian banks and, for example, the West Indies. Yet, he stated, important and distinctive as these ties have been, the shape of Canadian international banking has been largely formed in the past ten years:

> The big impetus, of course, has come from the tremen-
> dous broadening of world trade and financial relation-
> ships, the spread of international corporate activities,
> and, above all, the rapid growth of the Euro-dollar mar-
> ket centred in London. Since 1960 the foreign currency
> assets of the Canadian chartered banks have almost quin-
> tupled, rising from $2.7 billion to $13.5 billion [U. S.] at
> the end of June 1971, and they now represent about 27 per-
> cent of total assets compared to 16 percent at the end of
> 1960. Clearly these international operations now provide

an important source of earnings for the institutions themselves and they are also making a substantial contribution
to the effective performance of the Canadian economy in
a rapidly changing world.[1]

The economic interests of Canada and Canadian corporations
are significant to the nations of the Commonwealth Caribbean. But
to Canada and its world banks these same interests are insignificant;
they could wither to nothing and no harsh impact would be felt within
Canada's economy or on the balance sheets of its banks. The Canadian economy and the Canadain banks are, on the whole, strong; the
Commonwealth Caribbean economy is weak. Bear in mind once again
the gross statistics: The Commonwealth Caribbean is not a single
political area but rather a number of nation-states, with a total population of 4.5 million, stretching over 1,200 miles from the Bahamas
off the coast of Florida to Trinidad and Tobago off the coast of South
America.
    Donald Fleming, Canada's former Minister of Finance and later
Managing Director of the Bank of Nova Scotia Trust Company (Bahamas), said in 1971:

Much of Canadian investment in the Caribbean is represented by Canadian commercial banks. They have been
important factors in the financing of primary exports and
in providing general banking and insurance facilities upon
which the economic life of the region has been based. The
contribution of Canadian banks and insurance companies
and other financial institutions to the Caribbean economy
for a century has been of enormous proportion.[2]

CANADIAN BANK LOAN AND INVESTMENT POLICY

But what have the Canadian banks financed? In its submission
to the Canadian Senate Committee on Foreign Affairs, the Royal Bank
of Canada made clear its intent to give every "assistance possible
to Canadian and other businessmen wishing to establish in the area
[the Caribbean]."[3] There is, of course, industry. But in the Commonwealth Caribbean, except for the extracting and processing of bauxite
in Jamaica and oil in Trinidad, industry rests on a very thin base.
Moreover, for both bauxite and oil, commercial banks act more as
recipients of funds such as payrolls than lenders of major sums.
There is, too, agriculture—that is, the single crops, such as sugar
and bananas, that are so volatile in world price. Here the banks do
provide financing (more will be said of this later). Canada's former

Minister of Finance chose to discuss neither the extracting industries nor agriculture:

> Although overshadowed by aluminium interests in Jamaica, Canadian private investors have been active in the secondary manufacturing field including participation in companies producing chemicals, paints, soaps and detergents, optical lenses, switchgear, packaging material, flavouring essences, macaroni products, metal furniture, lumber, sporting goods, kitchen utensils, and television sets.
>
> A particular area of concentration for Canadian investors and businessmen in the West Indies has been the rapidly expanding tourist industry. Over 60 Canadian companies now own or operate hotels or tourist resorts in the Commonwealth Caribbean, and approximately 200 Canadian companies are involved in the supply of goods and services to the tourist industry and in the design and construction of new facilities.[4]

Fleming did not draw precise standards against which Canadian bank loan and investment policy could be measured. He did not indicate how much of Caribbean bank deposit money was used to fund the projects listed. He did not indicate how much, if any, of company assets or trust funds were used for Caribbean investment. And finally, he did not indicate the extent to which the bank merely acted as honest broker bringing entrepreneur and investor together. In sum, all that Fleming said was that Canadian banks have had an interest in the kinds of projects listed—nothing more.

Perhaps some illumination of banking activity comes from the Royal Bank of Canada submission previously mentioned. The Royal, like all other banks, draws a sharp line of distinction between deposit funds and other funds. Deposit moneys simply cannot be loaned out on a long-term basis, according to the Royal, for deposits by their nature are payable on demand or on a short-term basis. Indeed, the submission continued, when money is very tight, it is impossible to provide all the funds sought by industry to finance production even on a current or revolving basis. The Royal drew a line of distinction between its commercial banks, which accept deposits, and its merchant banks, which operate much as investment companies using their own funds:

> . . . [The Commonwealth Caribbean] has in post-war years in common with most developing areas, been seeking long term money for development purposes in excess of the available supply. Being conscious of this need, we [the

Royal Bank of Canada], along with other partners, were instrumental in establishing in 1965 Roywest Banking Corporation Limited to provide term money for development projects. Since its inception it has made loans in excess of $60 million in the Caribbean area. These loans have been made in the form of mortgages on single and multi-family dwelling units, some of which are government insured, loans to manufacturing and service industries, retail establishments, office buildings and hotels. . . . Additionally, the banks investment in government securities, some of which were earmarked for development projects, and provide current financing for many of the governments in the area. . . . Our trust companies, in addition to providing executor and trustee services, also do some mortgage lending.[5]

The Royal was not alone in establishing merchant bank operations. Its major Canadian competitor, the Bank of Nova Scotia, also organized a merchant bank. It, too, is concerned with equity and long-term investment, but its size may indicate the relative importance of merchant banking to commercial banking, where deposit moneys are most important. The merchant bank does not as such bear the name of the Bank of Nova Scotia. It is called The West India Company of Merchant Bankers Ltd. Capitalized at $300,000, the funds were placed on deposit with the Bank of Nova Scotia in Jamaica. West India was in 1971-72 staffed by a single young professional working primarily in Jamaica but covering the entire Caribbean. As administrative support he had a single secretary. During his tenure of somewhat more than a year before transfer to Greece, the managing director fully loaned all moneys available, often in cooperative deals with the Bank's trust company.[6]

THE EFFECT OF BANK LOANS AND
INVESTMENT POLICIES ON LOCAL ECONOMIES

The Bank of Nova Scotia and the Royal Bank of Canada have been mentioned specifically for they are by far the most important Canadian banks in the Commonwealth Caribbean. They stand individually as major forces in the area's total financial community. In terms of their actions as banks, it must be said that merchant banking exists but does not loom large in the total scheme of banking activity. Simply by way of illustration, commercial bank loans and advances for tiny Antigua in September, 1971, totaled more than $48 million E.C. (Eastern Caribbean) or about $100 million U.S.[7] Unlike commercial

12

banks which use the moneys of depositors in making loans and accordingly must regularly report to governments, merchant banks operate as investment companies using their own company funds when needed; they do not regularly report to governments about loans made.

Traditional commercial banking represents the major Canadian banking activity in the Commonwealth Caribbean. By this is meant activity keyed to and having a measurable effect upon the economies of the island nations. With perhaps the exception of the Bahamas, international banking using an island's favorable location for block trading in dollars and sterling and offshore funds seeking tax havens are not economically significant. Billions of dollars may pass through institutional conduits, but they are other people's money and not money invested in an island nation. The Bahamas is an exception simply because of the density of international banking. At the close of 1970 there were 151 banks licensed to carry authorized banking or trust company service or both. Of these, 16 were major banks appointed to deal in gold and foreign currencies. In addition, there were 12 trust companies holding unrestricted licenses, that is, able to operate as near-banks.[8]

In the Bahamas, banking density has had a twofold effect. It brought a large pool of expatriate talent, about 200 accountants. Perhaps more important, it yielded $25 million to the Bahamian economy in the form of government licensing fees, salaries, rents, and allowances. The bank payroll itself carries about 2,300 employees, 80 percent of whom are Bahamians (the government's payroll is $40 million annually for 8,000 employees).

Canada's former Minister of Finance Fleming said of the Bahamas:

> [The banks'] staffs purchase food, clothing, furniture, and motor-cars; they purchase or rent homes, and employ domestic staff in large numbers. The banks and trust companies are employing audit firms, attorneys, engaging in construction, purchase and renting of office buildings, homes and apartments. They purchase office furniture, furnishings, postage, electrical equipment and supplies. They are attracting business visitors to these islands who patronise the hotels for the hotel business is not by any means confined to vacationing tourists. They earn large sums in hard currency, thereby greatly aiding the Exchange Control authorities. They use electricity, water, telephones. They employ all the communications facilities. From all of these the Government derives tax revenues. . . .

13

[The salary scales of Bahamian bank employees] are the highest in the country, and materially higher than those prevailing in the United Kingdom, Canada, and most parts of the United States. . . . It is the financial institutions which are largely responsible for imparting sophistication to the economy of this country, for they are the principal channel of contact with business abroad. They offer opportunity to young Bahamians to take preferred employment. They provide training in almost every conceivable way, through courses, on-the-job training, and day-by-day instruction. . . . They offer inducements to their staffs to study for the diploma of the Institute of Bankers and other institutes of high standing, contributing to the cost of tuition and textbooks, and donating substantial cash awards to those who successfully pass the examinations.[9]

No other island nation in the Caribbean is in the position of the Bahamas. No other island nation has the same payroll multiplier coming from such density. Yet, for all the nations, including the Bahamas, the question must be asked: From where does the money come to meet the payroll, to provide the multiplier effect, to hire and train local talent, and to import needed expertise? In a very real sense, that money comes from the island people, who are the bank depositors. On the whole, the salaries of the Bahamian employees are not paid for by imported capital but rather by the profit earned from loans, investment, or deposit funds.

It is deposits and loans that constitute the measure of bank size. The proposition seems almost too simplistic. Its meaning, however, is fraught with significance: Banks, in the sense that they are being discussed are not giants because of anything they own. They are not giants as an oil company might be for the rights that it holds over the subsoil. Deposits and loans by their very nature should be highly liquid. Deposits may be called upon, may be generally withdrawn on demand, and because this is so, loans are usually short-term. Therefore, banks are not giants because of ownership. Rather, they are giants because of reputation—that is, they are able to induce individuals to deposit their moneys in the expectation that their funds will be safe and available on demand. It is primarily from moneys on deposit that banks become giants, for it is these moneys, managed by the banks, that are made available for loans to individuals, businesses, and the government. Within the constraint of perceived reputation, the banks are controllers over the use of funds.

NATION-STATE INCORPORATION:
THE EFFECT OF CARIBBEANIZATION

The current wave of nationalism compelling island-state incorporation has not changed matters. Indeed, it might only have emphasized the point. The Bank of Nova Scotia operated branches in
Jamaica before 1966. Obviously, initial funds for buildings and equipment had to come from Canada. In 1966, however, the bank incorporated with authorized capital of J. $5 million and 25 percent of the
shares were sold to Jamaicans.* Four years later this was raised
to 30 percent, with the promise of 51 percent by 1975.[10] Similarly,
the Bank of Montreal Jamaica Ltd. started operations in 1970 after
taking over the interests of the Bank of London and Montreal Ltd.
The bank is capitalized at J. $2 million, 25 percent of which was
opened to Jamaican participation.[11]
 The result of Jamaicanization has been only a passing of theo-
retical equity participation. The bank as an international institution
remains in control; the management exercises control and is paid
for the job it does. The shareholders have an interest in the profits
but are not in an effective position to substitute their collective judgment for that of the bank's management. Moreover, the bank as an
institution has received, not for deposit but as direct payment, moneys
for shares purchased by the local populace. Neither the Bank of Nova
Scotia nor the Bank of Montreal is likely to lose by equity participation.
Their strength comes from management, from being able to gather
and use funds, for, as we have pointed out, the Canadian banks in the
Caribbean are world banks.
 Reputation, we have said, allows the banks to become giants.
But what gives a bank reputation? After all, nearly all of the Commonwealth Caribbean governments have either established state-owned
or state-sponsored banks. Why haven't the savings of the people
simply flowed from foreign institutions to those of the government?
If the answer given is that the people do not trust their government
in the same way that they place confidence in the commercial banks,
then another question must be put: For the good of the state, why
can't government mandate the people and by force of law transfer
savings to government-affiliated groups? Surely then the size of the
expatriate banking community might be reduced and new nationalistic
enterprises be created. Again, the answer can only be found in the
people. The nature of money is such that those who hold it need not

---

*The unit of the Jamaican monetary system was the pound ster-
ling until September 1969; it then became the J. dollar, which has
maintained parity with the pound.

15

place it in any kind of financial institution. One important commercial banker said, "They can simply put their money back under the mattress."

Canadian banks have become giants in the Commonwealth Caribbean precisely because they have been able to induce people to take their money out from under the "mattress" and place it on deposit. Any visual inspection of any Canadian branch in the Commonwealth Caribbean affords part of the rationale for its success with the people. The branches by appearance are solid, affluent structures whose employees are programmed to a modus operandi. There may be inefficiency, but it can only be called marginal. In support of this semblance of solidity is the ever-present and prominent world balance sheet of each Canadian bank. Enter, for example, the Bank of Nova Scotia in Barbados and there, centered on the floor, is the bank's balance sheet reading not in millions, but in billions, not in Eastern Caribbean dollars, but in Canadian dollars. It is difficult not to be impressed. Indeed, it is in part this very atmosphere that causes a person to seek out a bank, to become a client. Holding a bank account on many of the islands is a rather prestigious matter. Being able to write a check on a bank that has billions of dollars in assets becomes a mark of a person's worth.

One cannot discount the psychological impact of world size on a mini-nation and the people of that nation. Consider only the Canadian banks' foreign currency assets; they amounted to $13.5 billion (U.S.) in June 1971. Contrast these gross holdings with those of the largest nations of the Commonwealth Caribbean—Jamaica with nearly 2 million persons, and Trinidad and Tobago with 1 million. By January 1970 the commercial banks of Trinidad and Tobago had loans and advances totaling T.T. $266.7 million and deposits of T.T. $353.2 million ($2 T.T. equals $1 U.S.); Jamaica had loans and advances of £125 million, and deposits of £146.2 million.[12] Next to the gross figures of the Canadian banks' world position, the loan-asset positions of Trinidad and Tobago and Jamaica are not very significant.

Even less significant was the former regional Eastern Caribbean Currency Area (E.C.), consisting not of one nation but several: Barbados, and the Windward and Leeward Islands. In the quarter of April-June 1971 the E.C. assets were $73.7 million. Commercial bank deposits in Barbados, the largest and most sophisticated member of the Eastern Caribbean, were E.C. $197.1 million ($98.5 million U.S.) and loans and advances were $172.1 million ($36.8 million U.S.; two E.C. dollars equal one U.S. dollar). The total money supply of the Leeward Islands during the same quarter was E.C. $23.5 million. Total deposits in the Windward Islands were E.C. $74.1 million.[13] Whatever the strength of this regional currency authority was, it weakened in 1972 as Barbados announced departure with the establishment of its own central bank.

16

Let us look at one of the mini-state members of this federation, Antigua. Here the power of the Canadian banks surfaces and can be seen clearly. For the period ending September 1971, Antiguan commercial banks had loans and advances totaling E.C. $48,243 million against deposits of E.C. $45,027 million. The banking community, and this means largely the Canadian banks, had advanced E.C. $3 million more than it had available on deposit.[14]

How could this be done? How could banks lend more than they have available and still meet demands on their deposits? The answer again goes to the confidence people place in a world institution. The banks made all of their available funds, plus some imported moneys, work for them. Neither deposit insurance nor reserves were necessary, for the banks' name is their bond. A Canadian bank manager in Antigua said, "We think of these small countries sometimes in the same way as we do in handling the affairs of a medium-size company." The governments of mini-states become only one of many of the world bank's corporate clients.

THE PAST: THE ROOTS OF POWER

A look at the history of Canadian banks and their expansion into the Caribbean more than half a century ago may provide a key to an understanding of the status of Canadian banks in the area today.

In no small measure, Canadian banks obtained their initial thrust toward great size and have since maintained their position because of the purposeful policy of the Canadian government.

The first general banking statute in Canada was passed in 1871.[15] There were already a considerable number of banks in Canada at the time, and their early incorporation, by renewable letters of patent, had resulted in a distinctive development of the industry from the outset. The first Act was largely a result of consultations between the legislature and the bankers and was passed with little opposition.[16] The original Act had the same form as the current legislation, the Bank Act of 1967,[17] and was the comprehensive company charter of the banks. It has been suggested that the main reasons for the enactment of this general banking law were historical, Canada's recent confederation and the experimental state of the banking industry prompting a desire for uniform operation of banking with fairly detailed legal controls.[18]

In enacting the statute, the legislature included, as far as practicable, all of the laws relating to banking. Of special significance is that banks are the only institution named in the Act, and they are subject exclusively to federal control. Modern Canadian banking regulation, therefore, is not the result of arbitrary legislation or the general enactment of settled principles. As first enacted, the legislation was the product of consultation between the banking industry and the government. From the bankers' desire for maximum growth potential for their institutions and the government's need for effective control over the country's monetary policy, a common interest had developed, and this common interest has continued to exist.

By 1871, banks were the major financial institution in Canada, and the Bank Act resulted not only in more effective government control of the economy but also in the grant of a limited monopoly to the members of the industry practicing at that time. The definition of this quasi-monopoly, which is under exclusive federal control, is somewhat circular: A bank is permitted to perform such business "as pertains to the business of banking."[19]

Government efforts have indeed been directed towards the creation and maintenance of an economically powerful banking system capable of holding a strong competitive position vis-à-vis other financial institutions. The relationship between the bank and the customer (the depositor)—aside from the recently established federal deposit insurance scheme—has been largely incidental. The result has been that the five Canadian banks that hold more than 90 percent of industry assets are in an extremely strong competitive position, and it is a position that is reinforced, for entry into the banking industry is extremely difficult due to the system of nationwide branch banking. The government has benefited from this result by achieving more effective control over national monetary policy.

E. P. Neufeld, a recognized authority on Canadian banking, has placed considerable emphasis on the freedom of the closed circle of banks to shape their own legislative rules.[20] Over the years banks have not labored under restrictive legislation with respect to their borrowing and lending activities. Changes in lending regulations came soon after they were sought by the industry. Laws touching on bank liabilities were not restrictive, with the possible exception of cash reserve requirements. Incidentally, it might be noted that reserves may bear more of a relationship to short-term funding of government debt than to the safety of bank deposits. Thus, to the extent that cash reserve requirements constrain banks, they do so to further the interests of government rather than the saving public. Bank growth, in sum, aside from the force of competition from other intermediaries and general economic conditions, has depended largely on the innovation of banks themselves.[21]

They are now financial conglomerates concerned with equity positions as much as they are short-term-debt instruments. They exist to render full financial service. In 1871 in the new nation of Canada, banks as the dominant financial institution were competing among themselves for position, for areas that each could control. It was not unexpected for the maritime banks, that is, the Bank of Nova Scotia and the Royal Bank of Canada, to move with significant force into the West Indies. There were the links of trade, the remnants of which can be found even today. In Nova Scotia the most popular drink is rum imported from Jamaica. And in Jamaica, a staple in the island diet, at least until very recently, has been cod imported from Nova Scotia.

But it must be said that trade merely provided an opportunity for the maritime banks to occupy an area not taken by the then well-established central Canadian banks. After confederation in 1867, the maritime banks had to find a place for themselves; they were at a competitive disadvantage with the more centrally located banks. Thus it was that the maritime banks had to seek out opportunities that were marginal to their central competitors.

To illustrate, though the Bank of Nova Scotia had aggressive management under Thomas Fyshe, its cashier, it had not expanded into central Canada. Its one venture into Winnipeg in 1882 failed when the western boom burst. The experience gained from Winnipeg in grain-loan matters was used later not in Canada but in Minneapolis. Not until nearly 1900 did the Bank of Nova Scotia establish business in Ontario.

Yet, the same Bank of Nova Scotia under Mr. Fyshe penetrated the West Indies. According to a bank archives memorandum, Mr. Fyshe's attention was

> drawn to Jamaica by a friend in New York stock-broking circles, formerly in the Bank of British North America with him. He investigated, and thought it a good opportunity for the Bank of Nova Scotia and one that could be handled by the men he had on his staff. Similarly when the Royal started in Cuba, it was an intensely ambitious maritime bank. It, too, had pushed into Montreal (1887); it had gone into marginal areas, by opening in several British Columbia places as the mining industry began to develop the province. And its [Royal] General Manager, Mr. E. L. Pease, took a quick trip to Cuba at the end of the Spanish-American war and got in on the ground floor of banking there; his American friends, who put capital into the bank, helped him to expand there. (The bank got appointed Agent for the payment of claims of the Army of Liberation.)[22]

The general economic condition of Canada and of the "British" West Indies added a final factor that led to the penetration of the Canadian banks. By the mid-1880s the Maritime Provinces were

especially hard hit by a general trade depression. Pressure was exerted
to find new trade outlets. At the same time, the islands were in search
of new markets. Indeed, as early as 1884, for example, the question
of actual union with Canada was explored by a member of Jamaica's
Legislative Council on a "nonofficial" visit to Canada:

> It was said, too, that some of the other islands were even
> more favourable to the prospect. The next year "purely
> commercial" commissioners were here [in Canada] from
> Jamaica. The Halifax and Saint John Boards of Trade were
> petitioning our [Canadian] Government for reciprocal rela-
> tions with the British and the foreign West Indies. In 1886
> an official of the Government was touring the West Indies
> enquiring into trade matters. In 1889 the Toronto Board
> of Trade was holding special meetings to hear reports on
> West Indies Trade.[23]

On the West Indian side, the trade sought related primarily to
sugar and fruit. Specifically, there were negotiations in Canada in
the 1880s for reciprocal trade concessions to ease a hard-pressed
West Indian sugar industry. But in large part that problem was met
and overcome by the United States grant of preferential sugar quotas
to Cuba, the Philippines, and Puerto Rico. Only in 1912, 1920, and
1925 were there significant Canadian trade agreements in which sugar
played a central part.[24]

In Jamaica in the 1880s the fruit trade was growing rapidly.
Foreign capital was investing in banana plantations, and the government was borrowing for railway-building, roads, and irrigation. Accordingly, it was not surprising that the Bank of Nova Scotia found a
banking opportunity there at the end of the 1880s. Mr. Fyshe's private
letter book states, "We have been repeatedly urged to open a branch
there; but we have always resisted—principally because we had enough
to do at home, but also because we had the impression the Island was
non-progressive."[25]

Mr. Fyshe soon changed his mind. His investigations impressed
him with evidence of progress. He made preparations in the late
1880s to open in Kingston—at a date, it must be remembered, well
in advance of the Bank of Nova Scotia opening in Toronto. In this
statement of history, setting out the rationale for Canadian banking
activity, it is well to emphasize that the maritime banks were seeking
their own opportunities. They were not as such simply following
Canadian business. Rather, at times, Canadian business offered them
opportunities. And, in saying this, one other fact must be noted: The
Canadian bankers had scruples. Not every business venture yielding
profit was ipso facto suited for bank participation. So it was that

Mr. Fyshe said of the American syndicate building the railroad in Jamaica: "I regard the whole scheme as one of plunder, more or less."[26]

Yet just as the maritime banks hesitated many years before striking into central Canada, they also hesitated in competing in the Commonwealth Caribbean. Each initially seemed to carve out territory that was its domain. The Bank of Nova Scotia opened in Kingston in the summer of 1889. In 1906 it became the Jamaican government's banker for the island, and in the same year it opened two more branches in Port Antonio and Montego Bay.[27]

In the interim, the Royal Bank of Canada had been first into Cuba. As with the Bank of Nova Scotia, encouragement came from Americans. In the case of the Royal, however, that encouragement took concrete form. The Royal moved into Cuba in 1889. Three years later 5,000 shares of Royal stock at $250 per share were sold to a group of Americans. Apparently as a direct result of the capital infusion, the Royal purchased the Banco de Oriente in Santiago and in 1904-05 the Banco del Comercio in Havana, to be followed by additional branch openings. Cuba remained the sole area of activity for the Royal in the Caribbean until 1907 when it opened in San Juan, Puerto Rico, and a year later in Nassau, Bahamas.

Acquisition afforded the Royal initial access to many areas. It absorbed the Union Bank of Halifax in 1910 and in so doing it obtained a branch in Port-of-Spain, Trinidad, and another office in Ponce, Puerto Rico. A year later, efforts to buy the Colonial Bank doing business in the British Caribbean failed. But in 1912 the Royal purchased the Bank of British Honduras, and in 1914 the Bank of British Guiana. At about the same time the Royal enlarged its position by opening branches in the Dominican Republic and in Grenada.

By World War I the Royal and the Bank of Nova Scotia could be described as major financial institutions in the Caribbean. Indeed, their activities, once rooted, did bring them into some area of overlap. While the Bank of Nova Scotia extended to Jamaican branches it also set up in Cuba, so that by 1913 there were three branches on the island and one in Puerto Rico. Thus, by 1914 the Bank of Nova Scotia had a total of 12 branches in the Caribbean and the Royal had 37. No other Canadian bank was yet doing branch business in the area, although the then Canadian Bank of Commerce and the Bank of Montreal each had a branch in Mexico.

During World War I the Bank of Nova Scotia did not expand the area of its operations in the Caribbean. (It was busy with home expansion. It took over the Bank of New Brunswick early in 1913; the Metropolitan Bank in the Autumn of 1914; and the Bank of Ottawa in the Spring of

1919). The Royal Bank, on the other hand, greatly expanded in the area at this time. As its official history says, "The tropical region of the West Indies and Central and South America found under war conditions a highly profitable opening for increased trade." Accordingly, to "keep pace with this development" it established branches in a good many of the islands (Antigua, Nevis, St. Kitt's, Tobago, Dominica, Montserrat, Guadeloupe, Martinique, Haiti); entered Central America with a branch at San Jose, Costa Rica in 1915, and South America in 1916 with one in Caracas, Venezuela; followed up right after the war, in 1919, Rio de Janiero, Brazil; Buenos Aires, Argentina; and Montivedo, Uruguay. At the end of 1919 it had 57 branches in the West Indies (of which 32 were in Cuba) and 12 in Central and South America (including therein 3 in British Honduras and in British Guiana). It had thus added 32 branches to its Southern operations since 1914.[28]

After World War I the Bank of Nova Scotia reactivated its Caribbean growth pattern. It tended to concentrate in Cuba, Jamaica, Puerto Rico, and the Dominican Republic, where it opened several new branches. This remained the pattern until 1954, when it went into Trinidad. There then occurred another area expansion. In 1956 it extended its reach through branches to the Bahamas and Barbados, in 1961 to St. John's Antigua, and in 1963 to Grenada. In contrast with the Royal, and as indication of existing "spheres of influence," the Bank of Nova Scotia by 1963 had 40 branches in the Caribbean, 27 of which were located in Jamaica.

Considerable space has been given here to tracing the growth of the Royal and the Bank of Nova Scotia. This has been done for two reasons: (1) to indicate the basic "spheres of influence" each developed; (2) to emphasize the deep roots, to the exclusion of other Canadian banks, that each acquired from before the turn of the 20th century. Indeed, it was not until 1920 that two other Canadian banks entered the Caribbean. Then the Canadian Bank of Commerce opened in Havana, Cuba; Kingston, Jamaica; Barbados; and in 1921, Port-of-Spain, Trinidad. In 1945 it closed its Cuban branch and kept its four remaining branches until the mid 1950s, when it opened strongly in the Bahamas, established five additional Jamaican branches, and two more in Trinidad—for a total Caribbean count of 16.

The Bank of Montreal, the oldest and historically the most international of Canadian banks, followed a quite different growth pattern. The Bank of Montreal initially achieved its international experience and reputation because of the conduct of enormous exchange operations. But with rare exceptions it has never operated foreign branches of its own other than in major financial centers.

22

It has, however, participated with other banks in such
banking operations. For example, in January 1920 it acquired a substantial interest in the Colonial Bank. . . .
The most recent foray is of a more direct nature: in 1958
the Bank of London and Montreal was formed jointly by the
Bank of Montreal and the Bank of London and South America each holding 50 percent of the capital stock. The core
of the operation consisted of 14 offices operated by BLSA
in six Latin American countries—Colombia, Venezuela,
Ecuador, El Salvador, Guatemala and Nicaragua. During
its first two years it opened in Kingston, Jamaica, in
Trinidad, and in the Honduras. At present [1963] it has
branches or agencies in Jamaica (2), Trinidad (2), Nassau,
Colombia (6), Venezuela (2), Guatemala (3), Honduras (4),
Nicaragua, Ecuador (3), and El Salvador (2).[29]

THE PRESENT: GROWTH OF CANADIAN BANKS
FROM 1950 TO 1971

From the late 1950s to the early 1960s the Bank of Montreal
veered toward a pattern in the Caribbean of direct holdings through
branch operations. It seemed to become more sensitive to the area's
profit potential. For example, one of its larger competitors, the
Bank of Nova Scotia, increased its Jamaican deposits during the five-
year period from 1957 to 1962 by more than 50 percent, while it funds
for loans advanced more than doubled.[30] Reflecting heightened business activity, the same Bank of Nova Scotia had by 1954 a total of
600 persons in its Caribbean offices. This compared with only 200
in 1935. Tables 1 and 2 afford a comparative statement of the Canadian banks in the Caribbean and Latin America from 1920 through
1962, and in the Commonwealth Caribbean in 1971.
    Whatever the Bank of Montreal thought when it took part in the
reorganization of Bank of London and Montreal (Bolam), it became
clear that the period of rapid bank growth had largely drawn to an end
with the advent of strong nationalism. Some writers such as Beatrice
Riddell of the Canadian Financial Post managed even in 1971 to give
the fact of nationalism an optimistic caste:

In the Caribbean where the Canadian banks have been particularly active for many years, growing nationalism is
nudging the banks to offer stock—and eventual control—
to local residents. . . . Royal has announced it will offer
25 percent of its Jamaican operation to residents in 1971
or early 1972, with as much as 26 percent more to follow

TABLE 1

Offices of the Canadian Banks in the West Indies
and Central and South America, 1920-62

	Royal Bank of Canada	Bank of Nova Scotia	Canadian Imperial Bank of Commerce	Bank of London and Montreal	Total
1920	97	18	3	—	118
1921	104	19	5	—	128
1922	106	21	6	—	133
1923	111	20	6	—	137
1924	107	21	6	—	134
1925	108	22	5	—	135
1926	112	23	5	—	140
1927	107	23	5	—	135
1928	100	24	5	—	129
1929	101	24	5	—	130
1930	95	23	5	—	123
1931	81	23	5	—	109
1932	81	24	5	—	110
1933	73	24	5	—	102
1934	72	24	4	—	100
1935	72	24	4	—	100
1936	70	24	4	—	98
1937	68	24	4	—	96
1938	66	23	4	—	93
1939	65	23	4	—	92
1940	62	23	4	—	89
1941	63	23	4	—	90
1942	62	23	4	—	89
1943	61	23	5	—	89
1944	61	24	5	—	90
1945	58	24	5	—	87
1946	58	23	4	—	85
1947	59	23	4	—	86
1948	57	24	4	—	85
1949	58	24	4	—	86
1950	58	25	3	—	86
1951	58	25	3	—	86
1952	59	28	3	—	90
1953	66	28	3	—	97
1954	67	30	3	—	100
1955	70	33	3	—	106
1956	71	34	4	—	109
1957	78	37	5	—	120
1958	83	38	5	14	140
1959	91	40	9	20	160
1960	73	35	10	25	143
1961	77	38	11	26	152
1962	79	39	16	28	162

Note: The number of offices includes sub-branches.

Source: Bank of Nova Scotia, 1963.

TABLE 2

Banks in the Caribbean

	Bank of Nova Scotia	Canada Imperial Bank of Commerce	Royal Bank of Canada	Bank of Montreal
Antigua	1	1	1	—
Bahamas	5	5	12	2
Barbados	5	5	6	—
Grenada	2	2	2	—
Jamaica	27	9	5	2
Tobago	1	1	1	—
Trinidad	11	10	7	—

	Canadian Bank of Commerce Trust Co.	Royal Bank of Canada Trust	Bank of Nova Scotia Trust	West Indies Trust Co.
Antigua	—	—	—	—
Bahamas	—	—	1	1
Barbados	1	1	—	—
Grenada	—	—	—	—
Jamaica	1	1	1	—
Tobago	—	—	—	—
Trinidad	1	1	—	—

Source: Bank Directory of Canada, June 1971, approved by The Canadian Bankers' Association.

within five years. Bank of Montreal has made a commitment to "go public" in Jamaica. . . . This trend will accelerate throughout the Caribbean—with Trinidad the probable next target for local participation. . . . Bank of Montreal was prevented from taking up an option on a Trinidad branch during the reorganization of the Bank of London and Montreal.[31]

But nationalism is a central fact for each of the island nations constituting what had been the Commonwealth Caribbean. And nationalism demands the capacity on the part of the central government to control the direction and growth of the economy of the body politic. So it was that the Bank of Montreal found itself unable to operate in Trinidad. It failed to heed the earlier warning of the Trinidad government: No new banks were to be formed without its expressed consent. The change from Bolam to the Bank of Montreal constituted the formation of a new bank. The government intervened, expropriated, and formed a locally owned bank.[32] What happened in Trinidad is not exactly as it was put by Ms. Riddell; the Bank of Montreal was more than prevented from establishing a branch in Trinidad; the government intervened by direct action.

Some Canadian bankers point with pride to the Bank of Nova Scotia, which partially Jamaicanized its bank in 1966, the first of all banks to do so. The same bankers note that the Bank of Nova Scotia was not compelled by the government to do this. Yet it must be asked whether the move made was more reactive than positive and aggressive planning. That is, did the bank consider it good policy to Jamaicanize? Or was it reacting to popular and governmental forces that simply had not yet congealed into formal policy? While the good intention of the bank cannot be doubted, particularly in the context of the effort made to conduct the public share sale,[33] so, too, there is little doubt that the bank was reacting to felt pressure. Indeed, the pressure could have been sensed as early as 1960. It was in December of that year that another Caribbean island nation purchased all Canadian banks doing business there. The nation was Cuba. Many years before, the Canadian banks had made deep penetration in Cuba—only to find in 1960 that their investment potential was taken from them.

For the larger and more developed island nations of the Commonwealth Caribbean, local participation, banks going public, may not satisfy the demands of nationalism. Moreover, even with regard to a public share sale, the island nations, like the banks, know that the capital required to float 25, 30, or 51 percent of any issue is difficult to obtain. The Bank of Nova Scotia demonstrated this in Jamaica. Other methods had to be found to give the island nations what they call the levers of control. Chief among these methods is central bank legislation, which will be discussed in the next chapter.

Yet, for every new control imposed by government there is a counterweight to be considered. It is true that there are more Canadian branch offices in the Commonwealth Caribbean than anywhere else in the world. It is also true, however, that those offices are funded out of the profits derived from doing business, and that business relates largely to the handling of deposit moneys. Should that business prove unprofitable for the Canadian banks, it would not be the first time that branches were closed in the Caribbean itself. It must be stressed that such closing would not dramatically affect the overall world strength of the Canadian banks.

NOTES

1. F. L. Rogers, "Canadian Banks Overseas," The Canadian Banker, October 1971, p. 1216.

2. Hon. Donald Fleming, Q.C., "Canada and the Caribbean," address before the Canadian Club of Toronto, November 29, 1971, pp. 26-27 (mimeographed).

3. Royal Bank of Canada, "A Submission Regarding the Role of Canadian Banks in the Caribbean Area," submitted to the Standing Canadian Committee on Foreign Affairs, January 22, 1970, p. 5 (mimeographed).

4. Fleming, op. cit., p. 5.

5. Royal Bank of Canada, op. cit., p. 6.

6. Interview with J. D. R. Laidley, Managing Director of the West India Company of Merchant Bankers Ltd., Jamaica, December 20, 1971.

7. East Caribbean Currency Authority, "Commercial Banking Statistics: Antigua," for period ending September 1971 (Barbados: Research Department, 1971), p. 1.

8. Address of Hon. Donald Fleming, Q.C., Managing Director, Bank of Nova Scotia Trust Company (Bahamas), before the Bahamas Chamber of Commerce, "The Financial Community: Parasite or Producer?", January 20, 1971, pp. 3-4 (mimeographed).

9. Ibid., pp. 7, 9.

10. West Indies and Caribbean Year Book, 1972 (Andover, Eng.: Chapel River Press, 1971), p. 268.

11. Ibid.

12. The Financial Times, May 26, 1970.

13. East Caribbean Currency Authority: Economic and Financial Review No. 2 (Barbados: Research Department, 1971), pp. 1-2.

14. East Caribbean Currency Authority, op. cit., pp. 1-2.

15. The Dominion Banking Act, 1871, 34 Vict., c. 5 (Can.). The banks had also received special attention in the British North America Act which provided that the legislative authority concerning banking, incorporation of banks, and the issuance of paper money would be vested exclusively in the Parliament of Canada. 30 Vict., c. 3, Section 91.15 (Can. 1867).

16. See I. Baxter, The Law of Banking and the Canadian Banking Act (Toronto: Carswell Co., 1968, 2nd ed.), pp. 1-5; A. Jamieson, Chartered Banking in Canada (Toronto: Ryerson Press, 1953), pp. 3-16.

17. Can. Stat. c. 87 (1967).

18. Baxter, op. cit., p. 2.

19. Can. Stat., c. 87, Section 75 c.e. (1967).

20. E. P. Neufeld, The Financial System of Canada: Its Growth and Development (Toronto: Macmillan Co., 1972), p. 111.

21. The regulation of Canadian banks by the Canadian government is more fully discussed in my book The Investment Function of Canadian Financial Institutions: Law and Reality (New York: Praeger Special Studies, 1973), Chapter 3.

22. Memorandum of the Bank of Nova Scotia prepared on April 23, 1963 (unpublished), pp. 7-8.

23. Ibid., p. 9.

24. Ibid., p. 10. In 1889, however, Canada did include the British West Indies, as it was then called, in their preferential tariff without reciprocal concessions. This gave raw sugar a 25 percent reduction in rates.

25. Ibid., p. 10.

26. Ibid., p. 11.

27. Ibid., p. 2. The Bank of Nova Scotia also opened in Cuba, but not until 1906.

28. Ibid., pp. 3-4.

29. Ibid., pp. 6-7.

30. Memorandum of the Bank of Nova Scotia, "Recent History and Present Operations of the Bank of Nova Scotia in the Bahamas and the British Caribbean," prepared by the Bank's Economics Department, April 2, 1964 (unpublished), p. 1.

31. B. Riddell, Canadian Financial Post, January 2, 1971.

32. The expropriation of the Bank of Montreal in Trinidad is more fully discussed in Chapter 5.

33. The public distribution of stock by the Bank of Nova Scotia is dealt with in Chapter 5.

3

THE LAWS REGULATING
CANADIAN BANKS
IN THE CARIBBEAN

In a formal sense, public policy ordering the conduct of global enterprises finds expression in law. In this chapter we shall describe and analyze the laws operating on Canadian banks, both in Canada and in the Commonwealth Caribbean. The statutes of Canada become important for two reasons: (1) The Canadian banks are chartered, that is, incorporated under the Federal Bank Act of Canada; as a juristic entity they exist only because the Canadian government has chosen to allow them to exist. (2) The greater part of Canadian banking is conducted in Canada even though the banks are world enterprises. Thus, in a legal and a realistic sense, the federal government has the power to control banking behavior in the Commonwealth Caribbean. Indeed, it may well be that the Canadian government has greater capacity to bring about certain banking behavior than the governments of the Commonwealth Caribbean themselves.

CANADIAN LAW

Canadian banks, as corporate residents and citizens of Canada and indeed as entities created by Canadian legislation, are obviously subject, in the wider sense of the term, to the laws of Canada which govern their banking operations and activities, directly or indirectly, both within and outside of Canada. Even if it could be argued that any attempt by Canada to regulate their foreign activities would smack of extraterritoriality and would accordingly be unenforceable as such, there can be no doubt that in view of the relationship of such banks to their mother country, it would be exceedingly simple for the latter to regulate such activity, by indirect means if necessary.

The question is, therefore, not whether Canadian laws can, but rather the extent to which they do, regulate the activities and operation of Canadian banks outside of Canada generally, and particularly in the Caribbean area.

A comprehensive examination of those Canadian laws that affect or have an impact upon banking institutions necessarily leads to the conclusion that there is a remarkable absence of any effort to regulate foreign activity.

The Bank Act

The Bank of Canada Act, RSC 1970, Chapter B-1, constitutes the basic, comprehensive statute regulating the domestic and foreign activities of Canadian banks.

No single section or chapter in the Act is directly devoted to or indirectly has the effect of regulating foreign banking operations. At best, certain specific provisions or features of the Act can be said to have an implied or tangential effect on such operations, but the overall and firm impression with which one is left after reading the Act is that its drafters did not intend to control the foreign operations of Canadian banks, or that if they intended to, they failed to do so, and, in either event, Canadian banks are essentially free of interference by the Act in their conduct of such operations.

An example of the indirect—and relatively uncontroversial—impact on foreign operations is to be found in Section 72.7 of the Act, which provides that a bank must maintain "adequate and appropriate" assets against liabilities payable in foreign currencies. The objective is reasonably clear, but the Act provides no clue to what is meant by the terms "adequate and appropriate," which are hardly capable of precise or totally objective measurement. It is noteworthy that this generally and even vaguely worded proviso follows the extensively detailed reserve requirements of Section 72 with respect to liabilities payable in Canadian currency.

Even less controversial or startling is the purely mechanical provisions of Section 73 establishing the procedures for redemption of notes issued by a bank for circulation in a country outside Canada: The bank is liable to redeem them at par at any of its branches in that country and not elsewhere (Section 73.1), except where it ceases to have a branch in that country and has not made alternative arrangements for redemption, in which event it is liable to redeem them at its head office and in Canadian funds at a rate of exchange specifically established by the Minister of Finance (Section 73.2). Section 73.3 provides that where a bank has thus issued its notes for circulation in another country and the laws in that country require or permit the bank to redeem the notes by payment to a designated authority in that country, such payment, if approved by the Minister of Finance, has the effect of discharging the bank's liability in respect of such notes. The foregoing provisions of Section 73 must be necessarily read within the context of the all-important—and overriding—stipulations of Section 75, which defines and limits the rights and powers of a bank generally, and in that connection provides, at Section 75.2.a, that unless the Act otherwise permits, a bank cannot directly or indirectly issue or reissue its notes if they are payable to the bearer on demand and intended for circulation; that is, if they are to perform a cash-like function.

In another and even less direct context, Section 76 prescribes, subject to certain exceptions, the maximum shareholdings a bank may own in a foreign corporation, that is to say, a corporation incorporated outside Canada.

The very first indication in the Act of the possibility that a bank may carry on business outside of Canada is found in Section 103.2, which provides that if it does so in the name of a corporation which it controls, and all of whose issued capital stock except for qualifying shares of directors is owned by the bank, then in such event the monthly return required by Section 103.1 shall be consolidated as between the two corporations with an appropriate footnote indicating same. In keeping with all of the earlier sections noted, this is again a procedural or mechanical requirement with no policy content or directive. In a similar vein, Section 105 provides that a bank shall, when and in the manner required by the Minister of Finance, provide him with a return indicating those of its assets and liabilities which are valued or payable in foreign currencies.

A final reference in the Act to the possibility of operations outside of Canada is to be found in Section 138.2.a, and it is, ironically, a disclaimer rather than an imposition of any controls in that it expressly exempts deposits or loans made or payable outside Canada from the prohibition in Section 138.1 of any agreement between two banks as to the rate of interest on such deposit or the charges or rate of interest on such loan.

Other Statutes

A thorough review of other Canadian statutes that in varying degrees affect the operations of Canadian banks reveals a total absence of any control, restriction, recommendation, or even comment on how they may or may not carry on their foreign operations. The Bank of Canada Act (RSC 1970, Chapter B-2); the Canada Deposit Insurance Corporation Act (RSC 1970, Chapter C-3); the Currency and Exchange

Act (RSC 1970, Chapter C); the Export Development Act (RSC 1970, Chapter E); and the International Development Research Centre Act (RSC 1970, Chapter I) are all utterly devoid of any reference to, or even recognition of, the foreign activities and operations of Canadian banks. Neither in the Caribbean nor elsewhere are such activities controlled or even scrutinized by Canadian legislative or regulatory enactment.

CARIBBEAN LAW

An analysis of the banking laws of the Caribbean host countries— and regions—in which Canadian banks carry on operations reveals that although there is a more intensive effort than that exerted by Canadian legislation to regulate such operations and activities, the net effect is not on balance significantly more effective. Because of the notable lack of concerted action on a regional, or transnational, basis, any attempt to exert more rigorous controls in any one jurisdiction would simply have the effect of inducing banks to withdraw their operations to the more permissive atmosphere of a more tolerant neighboring state.

Jamaica: The Prototype

The legislation of Jamaica is, of all of the Caribbean states under review, the most logical body of laws with which to begin, for a variety of reasons. Jamaica is the first of the states to have enacted comprehensive legislation in this area, and its laws quite obviously have served as models for most of those states which subsequently have proceeded to enact their counterparts.

It is also interesting, if parenthetical, that the two important Jamaican statutes in this connection, the Bank of Jamaica Law of 1960 and the Banking Law of 1960, were traceable in large measure to the study of Jamaican financial institutions and the resultant recommendations made in 1955 at the request of the Jamaican government by Graham Towers, a former Governor of the Bank of Canada—as well as to consultations between the Jamaican government, the Bank of Canada, and the Canadian Ministry of Finance.[1]

The Bank of Jamaica Law[2] was enacted for the purpose of establishing a central bank in Jamaica and vesting the latter with the powers and duties normally associated with that type of financial institution. As stipulated in Section 5, the principal objectives of the central bank, apart from acting as banker to the government, were to assume the administration of the local currency and of external reserves, "to influence the volume and conditions of the supply of credit so as to promote the fullest expansion in production, trade and employment consistent with the maintenance of monetary stability," and to foster the development of a money market and a capital market.

In order to achieve these objectives, the Bank of Jamaica was given certain statutory powers to control the activities of both foreign and domestic banks. Section 11 of the Banking Law[3] requires every bank in Jamaica to maintain cash reserves on deposit with the Bank of Jamaica of not less than 5 percent of its deposit liabilities. By virtue of Section 30 of the Bank of Jamaica Law, however, this percentage may be increased by the Bank to as much as 15; furthermore, the right of the Bank to vary the percentage reserve is exercisable at its sole discretion and subject only to nominal requirements of notice to commercial bankers of 30 days, publication in the official Gazette, and gradual implementation where the intended increase exceeds 2 percent.

A 1964 amendment to the Act gave the Bank the further right, subject to the same requirements as to notice and gradual implementation, to determine unilaterally the percentage ratio of liquid assets that commercial banks must maintain in relation to their deposit liabilities, such percentage to be not less than 15 or more than 30.[4]

The Bank is empowered, by Section 31 of the Bank of Jamaica Law, to require any commercial bank at any time and upon such conditions of timing and form as it sees fit, to furnish the Bank with any and all information that the latter deems necessary for the purposes of ascertaining whether that commercial bank is complying with either of these minimum reserve percentages.

Section 32 empowers the Bank, by simple notice, effectively to prohibit any increase in the total amount of loans and advances, generally or in specified classes, that commercial banks may have outstanding after the date of such notice.

The Bank of Jamaica was in addition, and for obvious reasons, empowered by Section 33 to establish and vary the "local assets ratio" of commercial banks operating in Jamaica, that is, the minimum ratio that the assets of such banks held in Jamaica must bear to their deposit liabilities in Jamaica. This power is, again, exercisable arbitrarily and is subject only to nominal requirements of notice and gradual implementation where the intended variation exceeds five percentage points.

Apart from the foregoing, which can be reasonably regarded and classified as direct controls that the Bank of Jamaica may exercise over commercial banks, there exists the continuous possibility of indirect regulation by the Bank as a necessary result of the exercise of the more traditional rights as a central bank given to it by this statute. There can be no doubt, for example, that the rights of the Bank to sell or purchase securities, or to discount bills, or to grant loans or advances—rights customarily given to central banks and, in this instance, forming part of an aggregate grant of such customary powers in Section 25 of the Act—can theoretically have a pronounced effect on the money supply, and accordingly on such areas as credit conditions, interest rates, and other factors having a significant impact on the activities of commercial banks, both domestic and foreign. However, these classic methods of influencing monetary policy can have very little influence in the absence of well-developed internal money and capital markets, and it is dubious whether the Jamaican situation can qualify as such.

The companion piece of legislation to the Bank of Jamaica Act was, as previously noted, the Banking Law of 1960. It was specifically intended to govern and control the operation of commercial banks in Jamaica, both foreign and domestic, and accordingly stipulates (in Part II) that only companies that have previously applied for and obtained licenses from the Minister may carry on banking business in Jamaica. (The Statute does not say which Minister, but it is presumably referring to the Minister of Finance.)

Wide latitude—on paper and in theory, at least—is given to the Minister, who is empowered, by virtue of Section 4.4, to revoke a license not only in the event of a contravention of law, but also where, in his opinion, the licensee bank is carrying on business "in a manner detrimental to the public interest or to the interest of depositors of the bank."

Although the next following section attempts to mitigate the harshness of this provision by giving the licensee in question a right of prior notice of intent to revoke and a further right to reply in writing to the alleged reasons therefore, this proviso is of somewhat dubious value in view of the absence of any right of appeal from the decision of the Minister, who, in the final analysis, retains the arbitrary right to cancel. In law and in fact, rather substantial discretion is intended to be vested in the Minister. Objective criteria against which government action might be taken are removed. In law, the way is open for the exercise of administrative or political decision-making. In law, therefore, it becomes clear that there is no right intended to be bestowed on the banks to do business as such.

Although the Act leaves the circumstances under which a license may be revoked somewhat vague and arbitrary, it is explicit and detailed in laying down the prerequisites for such a license to issue in the first place. Section 4.2 provides, in a clear if unstated reference to foreign banks, that the licensee must designate a principal office and principal officers in Jamaica. Section 5 of the Act further requires, as a condition prior to obtaining a license, minimum amounts of authorized, subscribed, and paid-in capital, and, after specifying these minima (£100,000, £100,000 and £50,000 respectively) empowers the

Minister to vary them at will. (£100,000 equals $220,000 U.S.; £50,000 equals $110,000 U.S.) Under Section 6, each bank must, furthermore, maintain a reserve fund in an amount equal to its authorized capital; this amount may be arrived at, however, over a period of years by transferring 10 percent of the annual net profits until the required equalization is met. By virtue of Section 7, a licensee cannot incur in Jamaica liabilities exceeding twenty times the amount of its paid-up capital and reserve fund.

The statute devotes much space and attention to an enumeration of activities or practices in which licensed banks are prohibited from engaging, including such customary prohibitions as the carrying on of a trade, the acquisition or retention of land other than under specific circumstances, the trafficking in one's own shares, and the granting of unsecured credit to "insiders." The requirement, contained in Sections 10.1.e, that a licensed bank may not lend more than 10 percent of its paid-up capital and reserve fund to any one person is diluted by an immediately following proviso to the effect that the Minister may generally alter this percentage figure at will, and by a 1967 amendment permitting specific exceptions to this rule in particular cases.[5]

Part V, containing Sections 11 and 12, directs its attention to the issues of minimum cash reserves and liquid assets ratios, which have been previously discussed.

Part VI, titled "Returns and Accounts" and comprising Sections 13 and 14, enacts minimum reporting and return requirements; for example, the Minister must be given a monthly statement of assets and liabilities, a quarterly analysis of customers liabilities in respect of loans and advances, and an annual return to include details of current operating earnings and expenses as well as other detailed information. For the purposes of implementation and administration of the Act, an Inspector of Banks, charged with the task of reviewing, inspecting, supervising, and reporting on banking practice in Jamaica, is provided for in Section 15 and the sections following.

Barbados

Banking in Barbados is essentially governed by the provisions of the Banking Act, 1963.[6] Enacted some three years after its counterpart legislation in Jamaica (a neighbor having many things in common with Barbados, including the same erstwhile colonial ruler), it is not surprising to find that the Barbados legislation reflects many of the features found in the Jamaican statute and, in fact, is a verbatim restatement of the latter in many material respects. Thus the requirements of licensing and the application formalities in connection with licensing (Section 3-5) are virtually identical with those of Jamaica;

furthermore, the same arbitrary discretion is given to the Minister to revoke a license if, in his opinion, the licensee bank is carrying on business "in a manner detrimental to the public interest or to the interest of depositors of the bank" (Section 5.4.c). (One oversight in the Jamaican legislation which is corrected in this statute is the designation of the Minister in question: Section 2.11 defines the term as meaning the Minister charged for the time being with responsibility for the subject of Public Finance. Unlike Jamaica's, however, this statute does not specify that only companies will be licensed, even though that is assumed throughout.) On the other hand, Section 6 of the Act, which has no parallel in the Jamaican statute, requires notice to, but does not seem to insist on approval by, the Minister of any corporate reorganization or sale or purchase of a banking business; the Minister may require, under the circumstances, that an application for a new license be submitted by the bank in question, but the section specifies that the existing license will nonetheless remain in force until replaced by a new one or unless revoked by the Minister pursuant to Section 5.4.c referred to above.

Significantly, Section 7 of the Barbados statute reiterates the principles of its Jamaican predecessor concerning minimum amounts of authorized, subscribed, and paid-in capital before a license will issue, but it raises the respective amounts considerably—to $500,000 in each of the first two categories and, with respect to paid-in capital, $250,000 (U.S.) for a domestic bank and $2 million for a foreign bank (or to use the statute's own euphemistic term, a "bank incorporated outside the Island"). Similarly, Section 8 repeats the requirement of the Jamaican Act of a minimum reserve fund as a precondition to continuing permission to operate, and it implies that this fund is to be not less than the amount of paid-up capital, but again it proceeds to escalate the Jamaican figure by requiring 25 percent of the bank's annual net profit—as opposed to Jamaica's 10 percent—to be transferred to such fund whenever it is deficient. Once more, however, the requirement is diluted by an immediately following qualification, Section 8.2, permitting deviations therefrom upon conditions which essentially amount to another instance of Ministerial discretion.

As to the types of pursuits and activities which banks are proscribed from engaging in, the restrictions and prohibitions are similar to those obtaining in the Jamaican statute, and indeed closely parallel those found in the Canadian Bank Act. Thus, among other things, Sections 9 through 12 predictably order licensed banks not to take their own shares as collateral or engage directly in a trade or industry or deal in real estate except under specially defined circumstances.

In other respects, the statute again reflects the apparent attempt of Barbados to borrow a principle established in the Jamaican Act and ostensibly to "improve" upon it by raising the relevant quantities.

Section 12.1.a, for example, prohibits a loan or advance to any one person or group exceeding 25 percent of the paid-in capital plus reserves; and Section 12.1.c limits the aggregate amount of unsecured credit issued to directors or other insiders and outstanding at any one time to $300,000 or 1 percent of the paid-in capital, whichever is greater.

Sections 13 and 14 largely repeat the provisions of the Jamaica statute in requiring licensed banks to file or publish monthly, quarterly, and annual reports, returns, and other statements containing specified information about their activities, financial condition, and other relevant matters. Sections 15 through 18 provide for examination and audit procedures similar to those relating to the Inspector in the Jamaican Act, for the purposes of administration of the statute and inspection and verification of banks and their compliance with the Act, with the ultimate penalty being, apart from stipulated fines, the prospect of revocation of one's license in the event of noncompliance.

Until 1972 no central bank exerted control over monetary policy in Barbados. The banks controlled by the government—the Barbados Development Bank,[7] the Barbados Savings Bank,[8] the Agricultural Credit Bank,[9] and the Sugar Industry Agricultural Bank[10]—are not central banks as such, but are intended and authorized to facilitate and encourage savings and loans to small businesses or specified occupations or trades such as small farmers or sugar planters. They are clearly designed to provide credit to persons and in areas from which the more conservative and tradition-oriented commercial banks shy away and it is clear that they accordingly complement, rather than compete with, the latter.[11] It is in any event difficult to conceive of these institutions being used or manipulated in any way as levers of control over the commercial banks. Significantly, Barbados in 1972 did announce plans to establish a central bank. It remains to be seen whether the central bank will be able to effectively implement the monetary policy of the government.

Trinidad and Tobago

The Central Bank Act of 1964 established the Central Bank of Trinidad and Tobago.[12] It is a comprehensive but thoroughly standardized and unsurprising statute, conferring upon the Bank the customary powers and duties of a central banking institution: exercising exclusive control over the issue and redemption of currency, acting as banker and advisor to the government, influencing and regulating credit conditions, protecting and encouraging monetary stability and economic growth, and carrying on useful research. The Bank is accordingly clothed with the normal powers of purchasing and selling treasury bills and securities; purchasing, selling and discounting bills and notes; underwriting government loans, and otherwise acting in such a way as to influence the money supply and hence such related matters as credit availability and interest rate (Section 36). The impact of this control over monetary policy and conditions upon commercial banks is, as in Jamaica, indirect and, although potentially significant, of limited consequence in an economic environment in which the money and capital markets and other components of the financial system are relatively undeveloped.

Sections 38 through 44 of the Act enunciate the nature of the Bank's relationship with commercial banks, on whose behalf it may act as banker. The controls exercisable by the Bank are more direct in this context, but are again standard practice: setting the Bank rate; determining minimum cash reserve ratios in relation to deposit liabilities, with a statutory floor of 5 percent; exercising the right to compel commercial banks to furnish sufficient information in order to establish compliance or noncompliance with these norms (Section 54, in fact, gives the Bank power to compel such disclosure for any purpose under the Act); with the approval of the Minister of Finance and after consultation with the commercial banks and the Minister of Finance, limiting the availability and volume of credit where the Bank wishes to exert antiinflationary pressure; fixing the maximum amount of working balances that commercial banks may hold in all or in specified foreign currency; and determining the "local assets" ratio of such banks, as that term is defined above. The affinity of these provisions with their counterparts in the Jamaican statute is immediately evident and their influence over commercial banks is presumably subject to the same comments and reservations made in connection with Jamaica.

The Banking Act of 1964 is, similarly, the companion piece of legislation to the Central Bank Act and again parallels and imitates its Jamaican and Barbados predecessors in most respects.[13] Its full title, "An Act to Make Provision for the Licensing of Commercial Banks and for Regulating the Business of Banking," is highly candid of its objective; whether that is its effect is quite another matter.

Illustrative of its debt to the draftsmen of the Jamaican and Barbados statutes, the Act, again with some variations in quantities or emphasis or other details of an essentially minor nature, reiterates the latters' provision regarding the need to obtain a license (Sections 3, 4, and 5), the requirements concerning authorized, subscribed, and paid-in capital (Section 4 and 5—respectively, $500,000, $300,000, and $200,000 or 30 percent of authorized capital, whichever is greater), prohibited activities and undertakings (Section 14), minimum reserve funds (Section 15), maximum liabilities (Section 16), "liquid assets ratio" (Section 17.2), creation of the office of Inspector of Banks for the same supervisory and audit purposes (Sections 18-22), and mandatory filing or publication of specified information, returns, reports and information at specified intervals (Section 23). Section 5.2 is innovative, however, in that it requires, in addition to the capitalization minima previously mentioned, that a "foreign company" will be granted a license only upon compliance with certain additional stipulations which are essentially procedural and repetitive of Jamaica and Barbados (for example, the designation of principal offices and officers in Trinidad and Tobago) but which also require such "foreign company" to supply the central bank with "such other information as the Minister or the Central Bank may require" (Section 5.2.e).[14] This is another example of the imprecision that seems to govern so many of the above statutes and their requirements, which are too often composed of explicitly detailed rules immediately followed by the right of a Minister or central bank to vary them at will.

It is also worth noting that this statute does not give the Minister the arbitrary right to revoke a license, that right being exercisable in this Act only in the event of any "contravention of this Act or of any order made thereunder," and even then being subject to prior notice, a right of reply, and, most significantly, a right of appeal to the High Court of Justice of Trinidad and Tobago (Sections 2.d and 9). Conversely, however, a revocation of license which is not appealed from or which is confirmed by the court must be followed by an application to the court for an order for the winding up of the licensee bank (Section 10.1).

Section 17 is of interest and is different from its prototypes in Jamaica and Barbados. First, it requires a commercial bank so to "conduct its business as to ensure that in the placing of its liquid assets preference is at all times given to short-dated instruments originating in Trinidad and Tobago" (an imprecisely worded stipulation which may accordingly be little more than a pious hope); secondly, the section empowers the central bank to prescribe the minimum "liquid assets" ratios both in terms of total liquid assets to total deposit liabilities and in terms of liquid assets originating in the country to total liquid assets, without, incidentally, specifying any minimum or maximum figures, thus leaving these ratios entirely to the discretion of the central bank.

In 1970, Trinidad and Tobago enacted the Exchange Control Act,[15] under the terms of which, among other things, only so-called "authorized dealers" designated by the central bank are entitled to deal in gold or in foreign currency, including travelers' checks payable in foreign currency (Sections 6-9). Conversion of foreign currency into local currency, or vice versa, must furthermore be made by such dealers only at the official rate of exchange established by the central bank from time to time (Section 10). The statute enacts certain other restrictions and prohibitions designed to fully control the foreign exchange market in the country. By Government Notice No. 211, dated 15 November, 1971, the following banks, among others, were designated by the central bank as "authorized dealers in gold and foreign currency" for the purposes of the Exchange Control Act: the Bank of Nova Scotia, Canadian Imperial Bank of Commerce, and the Royal Bank of Canada.

The Bahamas

The Banks and Trust Companies Regulation Act of 1965 regulates private commercial banking in the Bahamas.[16] In common with its counterparts discussed above, the Act requires a license as a precondition to transacting banking business, the granting of which is at the discretion of the Governor (Sections 3 and 4).

A foreign bank must conform to the now-familiar requirement of designating offices and officers in the "colony" (Section 4.3). An Inspector of Banks and Trust Companies is established by Section 8 and is given the usual powers of investigation and supervision with the corollary rights to have access to records and to compel disclosure. Section 9 marks a return to the distasteful provision conferring upon the Governor the right to revoke a license and to cause the licensee's business in the Colony to be wound up if, in the Governor's opinion, such licensee "is carrying on business in a manner detrimental to the public interest or to the interests of its depositors or other creditors." Alternatively, the Governor may suspend rather than revoke such license (Section 11). Curiously, the right to suspend can be exercised only by complying with the usual requirements of notice to the licensee in question and a right of reply by the latter, but the power to revoke is not mitigated by these requirements (however, the licensee may appeal a revocation or a suspension to the Supreme Court). The statute also provides for extensive powers of search and seizure by authorized persons in the event of any suspension of license or suspected contravention of the Act.

Antigua

The Alien Bankers Act of 1920 prohibits "aliens" from carrying on banking business in Antigua without a license from the Administrator in Council. The definition, however, of an "alien" does not include a British subject or a company incorporated in any of "Her Majesty's dominions" and controlled by British subjects and, accordingly, it would appear that Canadian banks are exempt from its application.

Saint Lucia

The Banking Act of 1969, the full title of which is "An Act to Make Provision for the Licensing of Commercial Banks and for Regulating the Business of Banking,"[17] is a carbon copy of the earlier legislation enacted in Jamaica, Barbados, and Trinidad and Tobago and examined above. There is the standard licensing requirement, the Ministerial discretion to grant or refuse a license, the minimum capitalization, subscription and paid-in capital (identical with those of Trinidad and Tobago), and designation of local offices and officers in the case of foreign companies. Revocation of a license is not, however, discretionary; it can only be effected for "any contravention of the provisions of this Act or of any order made thereunder" and is qualified by the usual provisions as to notice and right of reply; most important, there is a right of appeal to the Courts (Sections 8 and 9). In every other respect—the winding-up of a company whose license has been revoked, the prohibited practices, the cash reserve, maximum liability and liquid assets ratios, the appointment of an Inspector and the delineation of his rights and duties, the filing and publication of reports and returns— the Act is the same as that of Trinidad and Tobago.

Cayman Islands

The Banks and Trust Companies Regulation Law[18] enacted in 1966 is except in minor respects a carbon copy of the Bahamas statute of the same name enacted in 1965 and discussed above.

CONCLUSIONS

It is apparent from the foregoing that all of the Caribbean states examined have accepted the principle that private commercial banking must be regulated within their respective jurisdictions, and all have accordingly enacted statutes to that effect. Equally apparent, however, is that these statutes leave much to be desired in terms of this objective.

Although they all appear to have been cast in the same mold, there are significant variations among them, for example in capitalization requirements and reserve and liquid assets ratios. Furthermore, there appears throughout this legislation, as we have seen, a constant dilution of the impact of the rules contained in this statute by allowing variations thereof on the basis of ministerial discretion solely, with such discretion being exercisable in many cases without limitation by way of minimum floors or maximum ceilings. While the purpose of allowing such discretion may be both clear and honorable, it is necessarily a two-edged sword in that this discretion may not always be exercised in the best interests of the nation and may, to take an admittedly extreme position, on occasion be exercised in favor of a commercial bank which wields some influence on the minister or on the political party of which he is a member. The process of statutory amendment is far more immune to pressures of this type; in addition, the use of ministerial discretion should be limited in a statute because it effectively emasculates the specific prescriptions and proscriptions thereof. It is significant that no parallel to this phenomenon is found in the Canadian Bank Act.

As has been seen as well, some but not all of the states examined have enacted central banking legislation, but even where such legislation obtains, its influence over private commercial banking is not only indirect but of dubious significance in the light of the undeveloped capital and money markets in this area of the world and the ability of foreign banks to call upon the reserves and resources of their home offices.

The various regional groupings—the Eastern Caribbean Currency Authority and the Caribbean Development Bank, to name two—have neither as their objective nor effect a direct impact on the issue of controlling Canadian or other private banking operations in the Caribbean. Furthermore, and perhaps of greatest significance in this context, there does not appear to have been any effort by the various states to coordinate their banking statutes on a regional or supranational basis so as to establish uniform provisions and standards and to prevent the possibility (suggested in Chapter 1) of a bank avoiding stringent controls simply by withdrawing its operations from one state to another, more tolerant, state. It need not be emphasized that the Caribbean states are relatively small and weak and that the Canadian and other foreign banks operating there are relatively large and strong.

It is therefore fair to say that, despite the intentions and prima facie effect of the legislation examined, a closer analysis of its contents must necessarily lead to the conclusion that Canadian banking activity in the Caribbean is less subject to control by Caribbean legislation than it was intended to be or could be.

NOTES

1. See Ministry Paper No. 6 (M.P. No. C2729/88), Government of Jamaica, March 9, 1960.
2. The Bank of Jamaica Law, 1960 (Law 32 of 1960), as amended by Laws 37-1964, 31-1966, 12-1971 and 22-1971.
3. The Banking Law, 1960 (Law 31 of 1960), as amended by Laws 48-1963, 38-1964, 11-1967, 46-1969.

4. Law 37-1964, Section 12.

5. Law 11-1967, Section 2.b.

6. Law 45-1963.

7. Established by Law 48-1963, as amended by Law 48-1969.

8. Ibid.

9. Established by Law 15-1961, as amended by Law 55-1969.

10. Established by Law 10-1943, as amended by Law 51-1958 and Law 26-1965.

11. The role of the Barbados Development Bank, for example, as declared in Section 4 of the Act creating it (Law 48-1963) is: "(a) to facilitate and encourage savings and investment; (b) to assist persons in establishing, carrying on or expanding development enterprises by granting loans and other forms of financial assistance to such persons; (c) to assist persons in establishing, carrying on or expanding small manufacturing businesses and small retail businesses by granting loans and other forms of financial assistance to such persons."

12. Act No. 23 of 1964.

13. Act No. 26 of 1964, as amended by Act No. 25 of 1970.

14. There is a drafting error in this section, the intended meaning of which is clear but which does not make literal sense unless the word "furnishes" is added; as it now exists, the section reads: "(2) A license may be granted to a foreign company only if it [furnishes] (e) such further information as the Minister or the Central Bank may require."

15. Act No. 24 of 1970.

16. Act No. 64 of 1965.

17. Act No. 13 of 1969, as amended by Act No. 21 of 1969.

18. Law 8 of 1966.

4

A SOCIAL HISTORY
OF THE CARIBBEAN

SOME EFFECTS OF SLAVERY

The Commonwealth Caribbean has no indigenous people. Disease
or war killed the native Arawaks and Caribs. The Caribbean islands
began their development, their modern history, populated by slaves
who had been uprooted and transplanted from their own peoples, roots,
and history. For 300 years they were ruled by governments essentially
not concerned with their needs—physical, emotional, historical, or
developmental. They were ruled by leaders who did nothing to enhance
their sense of themselves as historical beings, as competent individuals,
in fact, even as human beings. The attitude of the rulers was summed
up by an observer in 1888:

> They were valued only for the wealth which they yielded,
> and society there . . . never achieved any noble aspect.
> . . . There are no people there in the true sense of the
> word, with a character and purpose of their own.[1]

Thus Caribbean society began with the great majority of its members
being taught that they had no value as individuals, no rights as humans,
no purpose beyond that of physical service. The ruling culture attempted to prevent them from developing interpersonal bonds by destroying the traditional family structure and by separating individuals
who had similar geographical origins. The environment of the society
provided only the barest support of its physical needs and, of course,
allowed no voice in its own destiny.

During the years of slavery and also during the periods of economic depression and slow social change that followed emancipation,
the majority of the slaves and ex-slaves were in a very real sense

nearly totally dependent on metropolitan or metropolitan-dominated governments. This kind of dependence, either cruelly forced, paternalistically determined, or based on the reality of being a small country,[2] led essentially to two attitudes or reactions—that of rebellion and revolt and that of passive acceptance.

There always have been some violent rebellions in the Caribbean. Some of this early violence is easily understood in terms of eruptions due to the extraordinary burdens and repressions of slavery. But rebellion only rarely was widespread, consistent, or even partly successful. With the exception of the successful rebellion for independence on the island that became Haiti, they were for the most part quelled easily though sometimes quite horribly. Among the more important reasons why rebellion was not more widespread was the earlier successful destruction of the family unit and the prevention of emotional attachments and unified groups of people, and one of the most important post-emancipation changes in the Caribbean was the beginning of the reestablishment of the family.

Toward the end of the era of slavery and after emancipation, there began to be more significant black rebellions. The riots at Bay of Morant were one of the most significant, though the reaction was in excess of the event. Such fluctuations and changes in the level of "acceptance" of their condition by Caribbean blacks can be partly explained in terms of the hopes that were kindled but were not satisfied in the aftermath of "freedom." However, some who have studied colonial societies have remarked upon a relative lack of outward violence and have suggested that this springs from the tendency of subject peoples to accept their presumed inferiority.[3] In the Commonwealth Caribbean, depression, shame, acceptance of self as bad or inferior, were the most pervasive responses of the population during the periods of slavery and initial emancipation. Moreover, during the century after emancipation, when one might have expected "big things" of a newly "independent" or free people, when this society should have been planning and initiating attempts to master the skills involved in conducting a free society, the Caribbean people found their economic situation impossible, and the reality of freedom extremely limited or limiting. Given this continued frustration and lack of success, what led ultimately to the changes that propelled the Caribbean nations into the active search for true independence and self-rule?

Theorists have talked for years about the fact that the dependency or complacency engendered in colonial relationships really mitigates against the development of technological and economic progress.[4] Progress socially or economically does not occur simply because contact between a greater and lesser developed society occurs. Rather, certain situations must prevail in the case of a dominated or recently dominated society before change can occur.

Among the most important precedents to change are (1) tension (psychological or political and/or economic, etc.); (2) the existence of creative rather than authoritarian individuals; and (3) the occurrence of a "revolution of rising expectations." William Demas states:

"The Caribbean by reason of its long historical association with the Western world and its close proximity to the North American continent, has been overtaken—perhaps more than most other areas—by a revolution of rising expectations. . . . There is a widespread desire for many of the more expensive consumer goods . . . increasing demands being made for the provision of expanded and improved governmental welfare services."[5]

COLONIAL RULE AND BLACK POWER

As a result of this revolution of rising expectations and the tensions produced by the dissatisfactions of 19th-century Caribbean life—emotional, political, and economic—and because the passage of time brought increased experience, change did indeed occur. These circumstances of tension and change provided the environment in which certain individuals, whom the sociologists call "creative," could develop and influence the direction of events leading toward progress for the Caribbean.[6] This progress was foretold as early as 1839 by a Jamaican:

The African race must ultimately become dominant in the West Indies. . . . It cannot be said that there is any impossibility in the European landowner continuing to cultivate his estates, and enjoy the profits of it in security, though the great majority of those filling superior positions in Jamaica should be the descendants of the African race. This is to be sure the grand problem to be solved: this is the revolution which to bring about gradually and benefically will require the exercise of great wisdom and policy: and here is the high and honorable task which is thrown upon the nation.[7]

In contrast to the totally unremarkable pace of development in the Caribbean during the century after emancipation, changes after the 1930s were rapid. These changes were based in part on alterations in world attitude toward economics and colonialism. But they were also related to radical changes in the attitudes of the Caribbean blacks. In the past forty years, they have propelled themselves along the path of psychological emancipation from slavery and from a sense of inferiority and inability. This emancipation is embodied in the rise of modern nationalism, the importance of which is the key to understanding the goals, the reactions, the decisions, and the needs of the Caribbean nations.

During the late 1930s the number of riots, strikes, and disorders dramatically increased. It was not only a depressed economy that precipitated the unrest. There was also a worsening of social conditions and a growing awareness on the part of the masses of the basic injustices of their situations and of the striking differences between their lives and the lives of people in many other countries. While the specific issues were economic, there was widespread political and social frustration. Because the economic "masters" or antagonists were so often representatives of metropolitan power, the unrest also developed nationalist overtones.

Out of this situation of unrest came a group of leaders who skillfully organized and coordinated the economically distressed into a widespread labor movement. These leaders, some from the West Indian intellectual class, some from the masses—Grantley Adams of Barbados, Norman Manley and Alexander Bustamante of Jamaica, Robert Bradshaw of St. Kitts, and Vere Bird of Antigua—helped the newly developed unions make use of economic issues as an end in themselves; but even more important, the unions were able to express social and political discontent and an emerging sense of black identity.

This latter concern with identity and self-image flowered into a "Black Renaissance," led by such men as Marcus Garvey and his United Negro Improvement Association. The concern of the new leaders and organizations was the fostering of pride in blackness, a reemphasis on black African heritage and a rejection of white values and goals. A generation of black intellectuals, writers, and philosophers turned their attention back to the black masses and to folkways. They espoused a set of ideas that became known as "negritude," "in which the positive human vitality of the black race was extolled above the dehumanized, technically and materially obsessed conditions of the white."[8]

As the labor movement developed, it undertook a relationship with the political elements on the islands. During these years, middle-class professional people had begun to develop political parties with nationalist overtones and sympathies. The labor unions could and did offer mass support in exchange for organizational and occasionally financial assistance. As a result of these relationships, trade unions and political parties in the islands developed in close sympathy and association. In this way demands for social as well as economic change could be articulated and acted upon. Also, significant pressure was mounted for the extension of franchise and political control.

The response of the metropolitan powers varied. Britain answered the disturbances of the 1930s with a Royal Commission. The report of the Moyne Commission stressed the importance of British intervention in order to enhance development, and it led to the establishment of the Colonial Development and Welfare Act of 1940. Among other things, the provisions of this Act allowed resources to be poured into the British territories for improvement of welfare services, led to the establishment of the University of the West Indies, and helped change the climate of metropolitan opinion toward colonial self-government.

Jamaica achieved adult suffrage in 1944, Trinidad in 1946, and Barbados in 1950. Constitutional reforms were initiated which led to the progressive taking over by islanders of the legislative and executive functions previously maintained by the Colonial Office.

Such gains toward self-government underscored and enhanced the importance of the political parties and gave them the necessary power they needed to push forward economic and social reforms. A significant amount of personal rivalry, political corruption, and error in judgment existed, not at all surprising in areas where so little political experience was the rule. But on the whole, progress was made. There was a substantial channeling of energies for national purposes.[9]

Yet, even with the considerable revitalization of the economy and the increase in the gross national product, per capita income increases were not significant. This was primarily due to vast population growth following improved public health and sanitation in the islands. The relief obtained from migration was cut off in the 1960s as restrictive immigration legislation was passed in Great Britain and the United States.

With the unrelieved growth in population came the proliferation of urban slums, crime, charity, underemployment, and unemployment. Pressures on governments were twofold and sometimes conflicting: they were asked to stimulate the private sector but also to provide make-work and relief projects. Here again, the "revolution of rising expectations" pushed in the direction of both development and discontent. Metropolitan aid in the area of social service was a positive response at this point, although it, too, had many critics.

The ultimate issues of independence and resolution of colonial status were not solved anywhere in the islands until after the 1960s. In many areas the problem is not yet resolved as the islands grapple with the concerns of smallness and poverty. Independence for the smaller islands at this point could in reality become only quasi-colonial dependency.

THE ATTEMPT AT FEDERATION

One of the first efforts made toward independent functioning
was a federation attempted by the British territories. Discussion of
such a federation began in the 1940s and continued to 1957, when the
West Indian and United Kingdom governments agreed to set up a Federal
Government of the West Indies. The outcome of the proposals made
by the Standing Federation Committee was an unusually weak central
government with a small annual budget, no powers to tax, no stamp,
no coinage, nor any agreement concerning the free movement of people
within Federation territories. The federal government established
in 1958 was a "triumph of the sentiments of insularity over those of
nationalism."[10] This federation, designed supposedly to provide the
West Indies with the degree of self-sufficiency necessary for dominion
status, collapsed in 1962, the year it presumably was to achieve independence. Many factors contributed to the collapse, among the most
important being the rivalry of two very strong leaders (Manley and
Bustamante); the centuries of tradition of colonial fragmentation; the
lack of amalgamation in the islands of the multiplicity of cultures and
races; and the imbalance in size between the two large units of the
federation (Jamaica and Trinidad) and the eight smaller units.

In Britain, changes in sentiment against colonial status continued
to develop, and this factor, coupled with the relative emerging strength
of the islands, led to the independence of Jamaica and of Trinidad and
Tobago in August 1962. Guyana and Barbados became independent in
1966, and the Bahamas in 1973.

NATIONALISM TODAY

The most pervasive and relevant feature of the Caribbean today
is the continued nationalist spirit. It is a spirit that can irritate and
strain the "delicate" relationships with the colonial metropolitan
powers. There is anger, considerable anger, toward the "mother"
countries, understandable in part.

There is a developing and continuing emphasis on rejection of
metropolitan white values, habits, and systems—all that represents
or reminds the Caribbean peoples of the centuries of dependence,
servitude, and pain. The order of the day is black, the development
of an independent, adult, black identity. This identity is new. It is
strong in some areas, tenuous in others. It is sometimes over-
emphasized, and its goals and methods are occasionally questionable.
But it is nevertheless emerging and insisting in its emergence that
it be accorded respect. The waverings, the excesses, the touchiness,
the growing pains of these states are all indications of a striving
toward maturity and independence.

FUTURE RELATIONSHIPS

Through most of their history in the Caribbean, the "mother countries" were punitive, repressive, and uncaring of the black and colored populations. Recent decades have brought what Eric Erikson speaks of as the "revolution of awareness" and what Gandhi called the "awakening from . . . the 'fourfold ruin' wrought by colonization in any form: political and economic, as well as cultural and spiritual ruin."[11]

How then should the erstwhile "mother countries" now respond? What role in the lives of these new states should the metropolitan powers play? These are not questions that can be answered definitively. Perhaps the most inclusive approach was suggested by Erikson when he wrote:

> At this point, we are beyond the question . . . of how a re-
> morseful or scared colonist may dispense corrective wel-
> fare in order to appease the need for a wider identity.
> The problem is rather how he includes himself in the wider
> pattern, for a more inclusive identity is a development by
> which two groups who previously had come to depend on
> each other's negative identities (by living in the tradi-
> tional situation of mutual enmity or in a symbiotic accom-
> modation to one-sided exploitations) join their identities
> in such a way that new potentials are activated in both.[12]

It is perhaps in such a process of mutual enhancement that independence and identity can be achieved by the Caribbean states, for the "problem of adulthood is how to take care of those to whom one finds oneself committed as one emerges from the identity period, and to whom one now owes their identity."[13]

What has been said of the erstwhile "mother countries" applies as well to Canada and its banks. In a very real sense Canada has become a substitute for Great Britain. Great Britain has removed itself from the intensity of involvement typical of years past in the Commonwealth Caribbean. Immigration from the West Indies to Great Britain has been halted. The purchase by Great Britain of agricultural foods will to some extent in the future be controlled by the Common Market. Canada, on the other hand, is increasing its trade with the Commonwealth Caribbean; the area is recognized as a "special area" for the grant of foreign aid; and West Indians regularly migrate to Canada.

The banks of Canada are in fact an extension of the Canadian state. Their status, indeed even the status of single banks on some of the island states, rises to the level of quasi-sovereign. It is not without some meaning that one of the most important Canadian banks has as its managing director of trust operations in the Caribbean a former federal Minister of Finance. Nor is it without meaning that the Canadian banks have achieved their capacity for worldwide operations precisely because the federal government of Canada as a matter of discretion chose to allow the industry of banking to become dominant and for relatively few institutions to occupy the field of banking.

Specifically applied, the conclusion reached in this chapter amounts to a challenge to Canada and its banks: In the context of emerging nationalism, Canada and its banks must find a role for themselves if they want to remain in the Commonwealth Caribbean. That role must harmonize with the aspirations of the island nations, otherwise the role will not be allowed to be played.

There also is a choice for Canada and its banks: they may decide to play no role, to remove themselves. The costs, the dangers, in trying to succeed may not be worth the potential reward. After all, the Commonwealth Caribbean on the whole is neither a rich nor a populous area. The next chapter more specifically focuses upon the views of the decision-makers, upon government, the banks, and the people. Out of a consideration of those views should come a better understanding of the "interest" conflicts that must be resolved for the fashioning of any role.

NOTES

1. P. Sherlock, West Indies (New York: Walker, 1966), pp. 7, 10.

2. W. Demas, The Economics of Development in Small Countries, with Special Reference to the Caribbean (Montreal: McGill University Press, 1965), pp. 90-91.

3. H. Bienen, Violence and Social Change (Chicago: University of Chicago Press, 1968), p. 52.

4. E. Hagen, On The Theory of Social Change: How Economic Growth Begins (Illinois: The Dorsey Press, 1962), pp. 19, 35.

5. Demas, op. cit., pp. 96-98.

6. Ibid., p. 97: "The predominant characteristics of such creative people are openness to experience, the tendency to perceive phenomena as being explainable, the ability to be free and imaginative with one's thought processes, possessing intelligence, energy and drive. This is in contrast to the authoritarian personality who in this specific sense of the word is an individual who perceives the world as arbitrary, capricious, painful and who is uncertain, dependent, deferential and anxious."

7. Ibid., p. 76.

8. D. Waddell, <u>The West Indies and the Guianas</u> (Englewood Cliffs, N.J.: Prentice-Hall, 1967), p. 111.

9. Ibid., pp. 123-124.

10. Sherlock, op. cit., p. 89.

11. E. Erikson, <u>Identity, Youth and Crisis</u> (New York: W. W. Norton, 1968), p. 296.

12. Ibid., pp. 315-316.

13. Ibid., p. 33.

5

THE VIEWS OF
THE DECISION-MAKERS

This chapter reports the opinions of the relevant interest groups as given in interviews. Government officials, bankers, business people, and students were asked to define the problems and approaches to banking in the nation-states of the Commonwealth Caribbean.

The land mass and the population of the Commonwealth Caribbean are not great. It is possible to speak with those in positions of authority, those able to make decisions, for the administrative infrastructure is thin. There need not be concern with sampling techniques. Both the governments and the bankers are accessible. So it was that a plan of in-depth interviews was devised. In total, nearly 200 in-depth interviews were conducted in Canada and in the Commonwealth Caribbean. This chapter is an attempt to summarize the thrust of those interviews. Names will be mentioned on occasion, but only where confidentiality was not requested. The Caribbean interviews, totaling nearly 100, were conducted over a period of three months in 1971-72.

First, interviews were held in Canada at all management levels of Canadian banks doing business in the Commonwealth Caribbean. The purpose was to obtain their perspective on just where the Commonwealth Caribbean fit into their overall scheme of operation and on the opportunities and problems offered by the Commonwealth Caribbean. In more than forty interviews there did come a view, a common profile, of the Commonwealth Caribbean.

The banks of Canada seem to view the Commonwealth Caribbean as a single area where they do business. Granted there may be special problems on particular islands such as Antigua. Still, the Commonwealth Caribbean is treated as an "area." Not infrequently supervisors are appointed for the "area." They do not report directly to the Canadian bank general manager but rather to an official holding a middle-range of authority. For example, there is, in essence, a loan officer overseeing all loans above a given dollar amount in the head Canadian office. The Caribbean supervisor, more often than not, would report to the loan officer.

At the highest levels in the Canadian home-office banks there is concern for the Commonwealth Caribbean. But there is not overconcern. After all, a single large branch of the same bank in Toronto or Montreal might yield more deposits and greater profit with less expenditure of "social concern" than all the branches in Trinidad or Jamaica or Barbados. In this context, at the highest levels of the Canadian home-office banks there is a general rather than specific awareness of the problems of the Commonwealth Caribbean, and there is creativity, a willingness to effect changes. At the middle level, at the level of the home-office loan manager, there is not the same creativity. "Banks," said one loan officer, "are in the business of making loans. Only good loans should be made. Ordinarily these should be short-term loans yielding a high rate of interest. And, of course, there should be the best possible kind of security." To middle management, loans that develop a country's economy are not as such the business of commercial banks; protection of deposit money, and effective, profitable use of that money, are the business of commercial banks.

In fact, it was only from top management or their designates that letters of introduction were written to arrange interviews with Commonwealth Caribbean central bankers and Canadian bank managers in the Commonwealth Caribbean. Without exception, the requested interviews were granted. At the same time, through the good offices of the Commissioner in Canada for the Eastern Caribbean Authority, letters of introduction were sent to the Governor of the Caribbean Development Bank, the Finance Minister and Deputy Prime Minister of Grenada, and the Premier of Antigua. Again, the interviews, and, as they proved to be, in-depth interviews were granted. Finally, secondary, supportive letters were sent by some Canadian academics who held or had held high administrative positions in the Commonwealth Caribbean.

Each scheduled interview was conducted informally and in considerable depth. Not infrequently the interview lasted longer than two hours, and not infrequently the government official in the course of the interview summoned key administrators to offer additional information or clarification. Either the government officials or the bankers often asked that specific information given be cloaked with confidentiality. Office interviews also led to other introductions and even more informal conversations conducted in a home environment. Another set of office and informal interviews were conducted with approximately thirty West Indian university students in Canada. Again, the purpose was only to prepare properly for interviews in the Commonwealth Caribbean. Yet, out of all the interviews, without exception, came a sense of nationalism in an area context. That is, the students wanted a Commonwealth Caribbean political entity. And also without exception came a sounding of distrust of Canadian banks in the Caribbean. Every one of the students thought it necessary for the Canadian banks to "Caribbeanize," yet they all had difficulty particularizing the meaning of the term "Caribbeanize." From some students, at their initiative, came other letters of introduction, often directed to middle-line civil servants in the Commonwealth Caribbean and to "Caribbean people doing business in the Caribbean." It was out of these introductions that there arose most of the home environment interviews.

GOVERNMENT REGULATION OF BANKING

Law is said to be the articulated judgment or rules of government. By definition, any sovereign state might enact laws to the extent of its power. No state need simply content itself with regulating its banking community; it could in the exercise of power nationalize that community. It would be a futile examination, therefore, to inquire into the potential of law-making power. Rather, questions of bank regulation must center on the exercise of governmental discretion.

Fundamentally, a government should ask itself (1) what is its capacity to enforce law; (2) will there remain deposit moneys upon which the law can act; (3) can the laws enacted respond to the felt problems. It may be useful to expand briefly upon the content of the three questions.

1. <u>Capacity to enforce law</u>. Generally, law is not self-enforcing. It requires an infrastructure to carry forward its goals. If a government should nationalize banks or create a central bank or an economic planning unit, there will be a primary need to staff the established entity. The less competent the staff, the less likely that the government will be able to effect statutory goals.

2. <u>Deposits upon which the law can act</u>. Both investment and deposit money are highly sensitive. If the owners feel threatened, they can withdraw their funds. Investment money can be transferred to another sovereign state with simply a book entry. The small savings account can be withdrawn and, as the bankers say, returned "under the mattress." Indeed, on the smaller islands of Grenada, St. Lucia, and Antigua, bankers estimated that as much as 50 percent of available money was "under the mattress." In fact, when the government of Trinidad and Tobago expropriated the Bank of Montreal it mainly took a building and the manager's residence—the numbers of accounts were relatively few.

3. Response to felt problems. Laws in themselves are not ends but merely instruments for the achievement of articulated goals. The more clearly the goals are articulated in the instrument of law, the more nearly the law will be effective. Law used simply as an instrument for wielding power will do at best only what is desired: It will take power from one source and give it to another. And it remains highly questionable whether the wielders of power are satisfied and whether their goals are met with the simple transfer of power.

Government must be capable of articulating felt goals if the banking community is to shape meaningful responses. If the banking community responds fully and fairly to each of the specific goals set by government, would the banks then be characterized as good corporat citizens? If the answer is no, then there seems little doubt that government has been unable or unwilling to state the terms and conditions for such good citizenship.

Whether government has asked itself the three questions, and what its response and that of the banking community has been, is central to the inquiry of this chapter. Our concern has centered on the expression of opinion. More particularly, attention has been given to the opinions of government, the banking community, and "the people" (a term that will be defined later). Setting out the opinions and distilling the interviews obtained has resulted in a two-pronged approach. First, there are the kinds of thoughts, the rationale, to which people easily address themselves. Governments can speak of the need to build an economy that will serve the community, and banks can speak of the need to protect depositors. But there are also thoughts and rationale that are not so easily articulated; there are the values and conclusions impelled by emotions. There are, for example, the problems of racism for some bankers, and black nationalism for most governments. For want of better terms, we shall place the first kind of rationale under the label "formal statement," and the second as "informal statement."

Ownership or Control

On the whole, the governments in the Commonwealth Caribbean have not been concerned as such with the ownership of banks. That is, they have not set out the goal of either nationalization or citizen ownership as a primray matter. (This is quite distinct from Canadian public policy, but it is in harmony with the present views of at least some within the Canadian banking community.)

The government have addressed themselves rather to the use made of those moneys that are under the control of foreign banks. Faced with a chronic dearth of capital, the governments would like to see the deposit moneys of the banks used to achieve government goals, which encompass the development of an economic infrastructure (such as roads, water and air facilities, manufacturing, agriculture, and tourism) and to meet certain social goals (such as low-cost housing). The economic expression of government policy is not difficult: Turn the bank loan policy from the short-term to the long-term. That is, have the bankers use their deposit funds for long-term loans rather than for high-return, high-volume, short-term loans. Let the banking community sacrifice a measure of liquidity, and a measure of safety would follow; let that community yield to a smaller measure of profit in the interests of developing a national economic infrastructure and meeting social problems.

The most rational approach to achieving economic and social goals has been the development of regional planning. In this regard, of course, effective regional government capable of making necessary decisions would have been desirable. Geography coupled with available human and material resources seemed to dictate such an approach. There are, after all, only four million people in a number of different island nations. Yet regional and even subregional government (the Eastern Caribbean Authority) failed.

The Caribbean Development Bank

What has emerged as a viable enterprise is the Caribbean Development Bank. Capitalized initially at $50 million—much of it from Canada and England—it has made significant developmental loans. Its president, Sir Arthur Lewis, residing in Barbados, sees the Bank as an institution concerned solely with the development of the economies of the constituent members. But in this regard, regionalism, he seems to say, must play a part. Accordingly, the Bank has favored projects that encourage the growing of fruit on one island and its processing on another. The concept is to maximize human resources. An island of 78,000 such as Antigua is capable of doing only so much.

For that matter, the Caribbean Development Bank is capable of doing only so much. The larger island nations of Jamaica, Trinidad and Tobago, and Barbados do not use the Caribbean Development Bank as the prime instrument for economic-social goal achievement. Rather, each has established its own central banking authority to control and direct the flow of dollars. Indeed, Barbados chose to remove itself as the dominant member of the Eastern Caribbean Currency Authority to establish its own central bank and currency. The result of this move has been to cast adrift mini-states such as Grenada, St. Lucia, and Antigua.

The Jamaica Central Bank

In Jamaica, under the guidance of a highly skilled, well-known, and respected civil servant, Arthur Brown, the central bank has been used to strongly aid in shaping policy. A ceiling was placed on the amount of consumer loans the banks could make. This allowed the government to place a partial check on the outflow of dollars. For example, less money was loaned for the purchase of cars. There was deposit money available and it had to be used or depositors would not have an adequate return.

Having created a dam of dollars, the Jamaica Central Bank then began to establish new channels for their movement. The Bank established a market for short-term government treasury bills; in essence, a place where the government could obtain short-term loan funds. This was made a permissible investment for the banks. Next, the government allowed the Central Bank to take short-term construction debt instruments for rediscounting. That is, the banks were permitted to buy such paper and rediscount it with the Central Bank. And the construction paper is probably intended to pave the way for the establishment of a mortgage bank in which commercial banks will be permitted to participate. It follows, too, that once established, the mortgage bank will concern itself with low cost housing, among other things.

A deep infrastructure is in the process of being shaped in Jamaica. Yet the level of talent needed to staff the structure may not be present. An illustration may serve to dramatize the point. On that rather traumatic Sunday in 1971 when President Nixon devalued the dollar, Governor Brown of Jamaica asked a senior staff member of the Central Bank for two computations relating to the effect of the dollar devaluation on Jamaica. The Governor's instructions were clear and the assignment not overly difficult. An hour later the senior staffer returned; he had been able to work one computation, but not the other. The Governor calmly said, "Come with me. I'll show you." This he did, and in fifteen minutes.

Agencies of the United Nations, the Bank of England, and the Bank of Canada have all lent their support to the establishment of central banks in the Caribbean. But the intensity and effectiveness of that support diminishes after the initial stage of establishment. It is a nation-state problem to ensure ongoing staff effectiveness and to ask whether it has the capacity to take on new and major assignments. If Jamaica with its population of two million is experiencing difficulties in these matters, what must be the difficulties of other island nations? But, one might ask, couldn't Jamaica call upon the banks themselves for consultation, even manpower assistance? The thought is not novel. Both Canada and the United States have consulted with the banking community extensively in framing laws that directly affect that community.

"Maybe so," said Governor Brown. "But why should we consult these bankers? This is our own problem. What is more, they could tell us little. First, they would have to consult their head offices in either Toronto or Montreal." Governor Brown seemed to be saying that policy is for government alone to formulate, that difficulties of implementation are a matter for government to bear. The banking community is simply asked to comport itself in conformance with law; it is not asked to be a creative force in the shaping of that law.

The Trinidad and Tobago National Banks

Perhaps recognizing some of the difficulties that spring from general bank regulation, Trinidad and Tobago uses its central bank along more conservative lines. It is an instrument to ensure liquidity and reinforce monetary policy. But, in addition, Trinidad has helped in the establishment of competitive national commercial banks. Two are presently operating. The National Commercial Bank came as a result of the de facto expropriation of the rather small Bank of Montreal in Port of Spain. It is established in essence as a Crown Corporation. Its president, Paul Rochford, former secretary of the Central Bank and recognized in the private banking community as a highly talented person, insists on independence from the government. This is done to give depositors a sense of security and confidence. Mr. Rochford's innovations come not so much in loan policy but in inducing Trinidadians to save, particularly those who are poor. He believes he is tapping a segment of the market left untouched by the private banks.

The second bank, the Workers' Bank, is one of three-way partnership involving the capital of the powerful dockworker's union, the government, and the people. Perhaps reflecting their newness to banking, the staff of the bank have a deeply felt social commitment and speak of achieving social goals through their loan policy. They desire, in part, to become heavily involved in low and medium cost housing.

"That may be their desire," said Victor Bruce, governor of the central bank of Trinidad, "but they will learn that their goals will have to make good banking sense." If Governor Bruce has his way, the Workers' Bank will be permitted to innovate just so long as deposit money will not be impaired.

The Associated States and the Bahamas

Trinidad and Tobago, Jamaica, and Barbados have all embarked on control courses that are familiar to North Americans. Whatever the defects of staff, structures have been designed that respond to felt problems. The same cannot be said of the Associated States or of the Bahamas. The Associated States in essence have been cast adrift. The Eastern Caribbean Currency Authority, though largely a currency clearing house, stood as the primary monetary authority for the Associated States. Barbados, the most significant member possessed of expertise, has withdrawn from the Authority.

Many of the Associated States now are fashioning their individual banking laws. They seem to be moving toward a central banking system, reserve requirements, and ownership and investment restrictions. Each island sees itself as independent and quite able to develop a sound base for economic growth without reliance—that is, dependence—on other island states.

Though mini-states, the governments tend to look inward rather than outward for a resolution of economic problems. Whatever may be the rationality of regional government, the Deputy Prime Minister and Minister of Finance for Grenada said, "We are not about to let Jamaicans come to Grenada and take jobs that our people can fill." With some exceptions, in the entire Commonwealth Caribbean there is a rather rigid system for obtaining work permits. Jobs are to be given to nationals wherever possible, and not to expatriates.

For the mini-states, garnering capital is always difficult. On the whole, there are no extractive industries such as oil or bauxite. What the governments do have is land, particularly for tourism, which often forms a major income segment for the economy. And on the smaller islands it is with significant pride that governments have announced "participation" agreements with new hotels. For example, in Antigua the Premier spoke of agreements struck in 1971 giving the government up to 20 percent of the equity, of the ownership, in six projected hotel ventures. This was given as a condition for doing business and, in that regard, obtaining land which frequently is held by the government. What the governments have done with hotels, they may well attempt with banks. That is, as a condition of doing business, banks may be asked to allow government participation— until such time as a majority of their island-incorporated stock can be sold. In the interim, the mini-state governments have followed a dual policy of both opening their islands to foreign banks and establishing small national banks.

In the Bahamas the small, government-controlled Penny Bank, in cooperation with the government, brought a Belgian housing interest to the island of New Providence. The Belgian group constructed a model unit costing U.S. $13,000. If, said the Belgian group, money and land were available it would build 1,000 such units—at a low but unspecified price. "What the government seems to be telling us," said a prominent Canadian banker, "is to make money available for low-cost housing." The Penny Bank, the national bank, was used as a catalyst to carry forward and dramatize the government "hint."

Nationalism emerges as a predominant fact in Caribbean Commonwealth economic planning. Each island state plans in terms of its own resources and expects the banks doing business there to be supportive of government planning efforts.

THE FOREIGN BANKS' REACTION TO
THE GOVERNMENTS

For the banks, good corporate citizenship must be made objective. That is, the banks must know in reasonably concrete terms what it is that government desires. The more objective the announced policy, the more precisely the banks will be able to shape a course of action. Moreover, they will play a reactive role. With some exceptions, the banks believe it is the task of government to propose policy and the task of banks to react in terms of the likely effect of such policy on commercial banking operations. To do otherwise would be to place the banks in a "political" or "interventionist" role. Some bankers, particularly Canadian enterprises such as the Royal Bank of Canada, have placed certain refinements on the issue of intervention and reaction. They have exercised initiative in encouraging dialogue with government and in offering the kind of assistance that could give government a sound base of information upon which action could be taken.

In his 1971 Budget Message, Prime Minister Pindling of the Bahamas urged a dialogue between government and the financial community. This followed some particularly sharp public comment about the need to do so by Canadian bankers. That dialogue, which took place in 1972, had but limited value for commercial bankers. The government's view of the dialogue is to convene regular meetings and ask if there are any problems. The banks respond, "not particularly." The meetings then adjourn.

Committed to conservative, traditional banking practices, the banks do not feel they are in a position to innovate or to initiate social change. Such initiative must come from government. Referring again to the Bahamas, several years ago the government began to build a low-income housing project, using what appeared to be general revenues. In about 1970 the project ground to a halt; most homes were left uncompleted. A major Canadian bank asked the government how much was needed to complete the project—its managers were willing to exercise that much initiative. But they received no response. The matter was dropped, for the banks were unwilling to do anything more. They were unwilling, in sum, to write a blank check or induce government to complete the project. What the banks would prefer is to have government lay specific projects before them for discussion. The banks would address themselves to the economic viability of the projects and the role they as bankers could play.

Of course, on a more limited scale the banks would appreciate open discussion of those matters affecting the vital life of the banks themselves. They feel that there is great need for dialogue on the nature of banking practice, the regulatory environment, governments as bank clients, private entrepreneurs, bank efficiency and the employment of nationals, and public equity participation. And they wish to discuss banking assistance to government.

The Nature of Banking Practice

There exists among a large segment of the banking community a belief that government simply does not understand the essentials of banking. There is a need to educate. That is, government must be made to know that: (1) the money on deposit is not fixed, but highly liquid; that money can flow back from institutional to individual hands. (2) Deposit money is not, as such, the banks' to do with as they will. It follows, therefore, that government policy designed to use savings for economic development should encourage savings. Toward that end, the ultimate stability of those savings dollars should never be put in question. Banks should not be encouraged or forced to accept high-risk, low-yield loans.

Regulatory Environment

Banking laws designed simply as an exercise of sovereignty can do harm to the nation-state by eroding bank strength. To government, the concept of branch banks may carry with it an inference of oppression or, at the least, decisions affecting the economy made by private, non-national entities. Yet to remedy the problem by requiring separate incorporation tends to bring rigidity both to government and the banks. A bank incorporated within an island state will have by definition a fixed capital base. Moreover, its loans will be geared to that base. Thus, a bank capitalized and having deposits not exceeding $5 million (a not unusual situation for the Associated States) generally will be limited in the amount and number of loans available, and will be required to seek headquarters guarantees for loans exceeding 10 percent of deposits. A branch bank, but not a separately incorporated bank, could lend in excess of deposits available in the nation-state. On the islands of Grenada, St. Lucia, Antigua, and the Bahamas it was not unusual at various times to find banks loaned out at sometimes 120 to 130 percent of deposits.

If new laws are to be enacted, bank officials have pleaded, at least give the banking community an opportunity to comment on them. With such comment, they seem to be saying, government can have a better grasp of reality.

Laws, statutes in themselves, only form a paper environment. The reality of a legal environment comes in the action-decisions that control bank behavior. Thus, the creation of a central bank in Jamaica had no particular immediate effect on commercial banking there. But when that central bank through the Governor placed a ceiling on the kind and amount of commercial loans a bank might make, there was a practical reality given the central bank; it did something that materially touched the private banking system. It is about that reality which the private bankers would appreciate dialogue. The subject matter for talk ranges from broad to narrow.

Governments as Bank Clients

Whatever the political climate or aspirations of government may be, particularly in the smaller island states, government often remains and is treated as a bank client. A banker in St. Lucia said, "Government is simply a large client for certain purposes." A bank dealing with any important client on an ongoing basis is concerned about that client's ability to pay its revenues and its debts—and government is a heavy borrower of funds. Banks would prefer to see government solvent rather than insolvent if for no other reason than to allow the banking community greater flexibility. A government hard pressed to pay debts or unable to raise additional tax moneys will turn to the banks as a convenient source of funding. What the banks would like is responsibility on the part of government. They would like to see government's fiscal house put in order. It does no good for the banking community to see the government of Antigua spend 25 percent of its budget to handle the nation's current debt, leaving only about $100,000 for developmental programs in a nation where unemployment is estimated between 30 and 60 percent.

Whatever the banking regulatory structure, the banking community feels a compelling need for discussion of government's ordering of priorities. Viewing government as a client, the banks want it to have a rationalized budget out of which could come bank proposals relating to debt consolidation and debt management. The preparation of such a budget not only involves skills but, perhaps more important, self-discipline and a capacity to induce self-discipline on the populace—for debt management may compel abstinence in the present for wealth in the future.

Private Entrepreneurs

The economies of most of the island nations do not have a wide base. Relatively few industries bring in most of the revenue, and any major project that goes awry could have a significantly adverse affect on the economy. Banks know this and they would like government to have the same understanding. That is, they would like to have government utilize freely available bank credit-checking services to report on those entrepreneurs attempting to launch significant ventures with government support. And equally important, as government tries to spur competition between banks, is the need for government to know just who will manage new financial enterprises. In part, it was the government's failure to heed responsible banking advice that led to the failure of the British American Bank in the Bahamas.

Bank Efficiency and Employment of Nationals

As the banks are concerned with efficient project development, so, too, they have a vital interest in maintaining the efficiency of their own units. The banks have agreed with and have carried forward public policy urging employment of nationals in the banks. They have instituted recruitment and training programs. Except for top managerial positions, most commercial banks now employ not only nationals but black nationals. The problem of the banks is twofold: (1) National employment policy is restrictive to the nationals themselves; it inhibits the freedom of many banks to transfer nationals to other areas. As a result, successful nationals can only move to the top of their own nation-state ladder and are denied a breadth of experience which would make them more able and give them upward mobility. (2) The first national reaching the top of his nation-state's commercial banking ladder thereby places all other employees in a restrictive position; there can be no further upward movement until the top person moves.

The difficulty does not end there. While Canada's commercial banks by law have had their relationship with domestic trust companies severed, this does not apply to extraterritorial activity. Each of Canada's major overseas banks does own and operate a trust company in the Caribbean. In several major respects their operations cannot be likened to that of a commercial bank. Although often permitted by law, trust companies on the whole do not solicit general deposit moneys from the public. Rather, trust company work involves the administration of large, complex trusts involving offshore funds. They have relatively little relationship with domestic trusts and estates, which in the Caribbean are often personally administered by individual lawyers. The trust companies have no relationship with the consumer of small loans. This business is handled by the commercial banks with well-programmed schemes such as the Scotia Plan, designed by the Bank of Nova Scotia "for the man on the street."

Trust company management is placed under the same public policy strictures concerning employment. The Canadian trust companies have initiated training programs, but the work is complex. To date they have been largely unable to import talent needed to get the work done. Work permits at best are difficult to obtain, and the application forms are archaic (in the Bahamas a transcript of high school grades is required). Where permission is obtained it takes about two to three months to complete the detailed form and another three to four months for government clearance. And the clearance, when it does come, often covers only a year. "We cannot hire a senior trust officer for only a year," said Donald Fleming, former Canadian Minister of Finance and now head of the Bank of Nova Scotia Trust Company in the Bahamas.

With inadequate senior staff, new trust business has been diverted to "more favorable" climates such as the Cayman Islands. Even existing trust business is being transferred.

Part of the problem, bank management indicate, is government lack of understanding. "You cannot make a person qualified for a job by simply saying he is qualified. The skills must be learned, and that takes time." Some bankers smile sadly, noting the Bahamas, where there are 300 offshore banks whose business is largely composed of "bookings" for dollar exchanges. They believe the Bahamian government intends to force Bahamians into senior positions in these banks. "But," the bankers say, "that will never happen. The banks will close their operations first. It is not that difficult to do. They can move elsewhere."

Public Equity Participation

In what might have appeared as the most sensitive and vital subject for dialogue, there has been relatively little desire or need for talk. Each of the major Canadian banks has committed itself to either significant local participation or control. In Jamaica the Bank of Nova Scotia, through strenuous effort, much of it outside the institutionalized auction market, did manage to sell 25 percent of their Jamaican equity and have announced a commitment to 51 percent. It is highly unlikely that either the Bank of Nova Scotia or any other major bank—short of intense person-to-person selling—will be able to cause the distribution of any major stock issue.

Government seems to recognize the limitations of the auction market and seems to have accepted the promises of equity participation as made in good faith. What is interesting is the lack of discussion of non-auction-market methods for causing equity participation. These methods do exist: (1) In Barbados, the banks acting as a de facto securities commission caused six issues to go public in a period of one year; they were sold from tellers' cages and were successful. (2) In Trinidad and Tobago a large, aggressive, and relatively affluent East Indian community exists, constituting a potential source of capital. For Canadian banks ethnicity is not new. The forthcoming Unity Bank is based on it. In the United States, long a watching point for Canadian banking, special impetus has been given, for example, to black-owned banks. There is a possibility for Canadian banks to go public in Trinidad through direct appeal to the East Indian population. (3) Finally, the Bank of Montreal is evolving a franchise scheme for banking which would permit small local (that is, national) banks in which control would be in the hands of nationals. Under contract only, in what would amount to a franchise arrangement, management would be in the Bank of Montreal. With management would come the right to use the bank's name and draw upon its worldwide offices and expertise.

Although the issue is important in the context of a growing nationalism, the governments have not engaged in discussion about equity participation because the possibilities for going public by means other than a formal auction market have not been clearly articulated. In part, too, the governments have not spoken because it is the banks rather than government that take stock to the public; the banks are expected to be skilled technicians. It would seem to be in the interests of both the banking community and government to see innovation in public distribution, for this might blunt some of the thrust of an irrational nationalism.

Banking Assistance to Government

Just as there are specific points on the banks' agenda for dialogue, there are specific areas in which banks are prepared to render assistance. It is no charitable gesture being made. Rather, the banks are concerned—particularly in a hostile climate of surging nationalism—to have a regulatory administrative apparatus that is aware of reality and of just how much the banks are capable of doing. The banks recognize, too, that a skilled administrative apparatus may not always be able to affect policy where felt political necessities may bear no relationship to economic reality. Indeed, this lack of policy input is quite marked in the Bahamas. But the opposite is true in Jamaica. There Arthur Brown, the highly talented central banker, does play a major role in shaping government policy.

The banks do not regret having trained personnel move from the commercial banking sector to that of government. The more sophisticated these persons are, the more likely they are to form rational judgments. Islands such as the Bahamas, Jamaica, Barbados, and Trinidad have at least some qualified personnel. The Associated States, cast adrift from Barbados, the dominant partner of the Eastern Caribbean Currency Authority, have next to no skilled administrators. In Antigua the Premier holds the portfolio of Finance Minister. His Financial Secretary, that is, his chief assistant, is a relatively young man holding a degree from Toronto as a chartered accountant.

On each island throughout the Commonwealth Caribbean, and on a world basis, each of the Canadian global banks can provide an infra- structure, without cost to the government. If government, particularly in the smaller islands, should attempt to establish a full administrative structure for the control of financial institutions, the cost would be heavy, and manpower would be scarce. Under the best of circumstances it will be difficult for Antigua to create a central bank and utilize the information flow into that bank.

The banks can provide manpower on a limited basis for some essential financial tasks. They can help to create the record-keeping system which would allow for the proper statement of government accounts. On some of the smaller islands government has been more than two years behind in any statement of accounts. Then what emerges is a partial statement of account two years out of date. On some of the larger islands major government-subsidized enterprises such as British West Indies Airways (BWIA) in Trinidad have yet to make a statement of account after years of operation.

With a proper statement of account the banks would be in a posi- tion to render significant direct assistance to government in the form of debt management and consolidation. In Antigua, burdened by a number of heavy debts, this has already been suggested to government by one member of the banking community, but there has been no response—nor is there likely to be one until an ordering of priorities takes place.

Tied to budget is the flow of dollars. In some of the smaller nation-states there are no foreign exchange controls. Some banks have suggested the desirability of instituting such controls, within limits, using the banks as enforcing agents of the government. Again, the proposal has met with silence.

Finally, as stated above, the banks are willing to act as credit- checkers, as a service only. Government can take the advice if it so chooses, and there would be no dictation from the banks.

Indeed, for each of the itemized points of assistance, government is not in a position of yielding sovereignty but is merely the recipient of information to make use of as it sees fit. There are only two cost factors: (1) Banks become privy to information of concern to government. (2) To the extent that information has restricted publication, government may feel inhibited from making certain decisions. So long as the banks are intended to be vital institutions of and within the state, neither cost factor stands as significant.

THE ATTITUDES OF THE PEOPLE

There are no current behavioral studies reflecting the position of the people in the Commonwealth Caribbean. It would be a serious mistake to posit any single profile of popular feeling. But it may be useful to point out that conflict can develop between people and their government and that within the population there may be points of vocal dissent that may conflict with the government and other segments of the population.

Among the mass of people there is no noticeable revolutionary zeal. A revolution requires popular self-discipline, a willingness on the part of the people to accept the dictates of political leadership. To do so may mean, as in Cuba, a willingness to forego consumer goods in an effort to build an economic infrastructure, and a willingness to accept uncomfortable, unpleasant work to allow the nation to garner its resources. It may mean the mobilization of the population to cut sugar cane.

From sophisticated Barbados to the more primitive island of Antigua, portions of the important sugar cane harvest are wasted because people do not want to work in the fields. Their refusal to cut cane becomes all the more meaningful in light of the high rate of unemployment, which in Antigua has been estimated to range from 30 to 60 percent. The cane of Barbados and Antigua was cut in no small measure because migrant labor was obtained from St. Lucia.

Yet in both Antigua and Barbados, automobiles, a high-cost import product, are in abundance. In Antigua, poorer than Barbados, persons often fly to Puerto Rico to buy large used American cars. They gather their personal funds and the collective sous-sous to make their major purchase. The cars purchased then become part of a massive taxi fleet used to transport tourists over relatively few roads at very high prices. A more rational economic system might recognize the need for taxis and personal cars. It would at the same time put some limit on the numbers that could be purchased. The result would tend to cut off one avenue of dollars spent abroad so that more could be done at home. And, with fewer taxis, there would be the opportunity for more passengers and more income for each taxi and at the same time the possibility of lower fares. For an area of the world that is rapidly overpricing itself in the tourist business, any move toward lower prices would be useful.

Only in the nation of Jamaica have major controls been placed on consumer spending for imported items. But, curiously, aside from Trinidad and Tobago, Jamaica is in the best position to develop a viable economy. It has some industry; it has bauxite; it has some tourism; and it has a large population base relative to the rest of the Caribbean. The less economically stable islands have the greater need to impose consumer credit and foreign exchange controls.

The reason for the different action comes from the facts themselves. Jamaica is, on the whole, strong; Antigua is weak. It is government that must determine whether and how economic restraints will be imposed. Government is responsive to the people; the fewer the number of people, the greater must be the level of government responsiveness. In Jamaica, government could more easily make a political decision to limit consumer credit. It has an administrative apparatus, a central bank, which could impose those controls indirectly. That is, the commercial banks are simply informed by the central bank that consumer loans may not exceed the level set in a previous year. It was the banks, and not the government, that had to inform the citizen of Jamaica that no money was available for an auto loan. It was a difficult task for the banks: How does a loan officer explain to two credit-worthy persons that one will get the loan and the other will not? Who bears the anger? Government or the bank-loan officer?

While the banks of Jamaica make fewer consumer loans, they nevertheless continue to gather deposit money which must be invested to keep the banks operating and to earn interest for depositors. With the money that has been purposely dammed, Government has created two avenues for bank investment: treasury bills and construction paper. Both go to finance the kind of economic development government hopes to encourage. In time, the government probably will establish a home mortgage bank in which the commercial banks will be urged to invest. The home mortgage bank will provide a market for the paper of house mortgages. But, it must be reemphasized, this expansion of economic activity has a cost which the consumer must pay.

For Antigua or Grenada, and even Barbados and Trinidad and Tobago, government may not feel able to make the political decision to compel consumer restraint. To do otherwise involves government in risk-taking. The risks are many: People would be asked to discipline themselves in the expectation of reward. In essence, the people—at their elected leaders' request—would be giving government time and money. Government, accordingly would have clear power and corresponding responsibility to bring to the people the reward of a better life for the restraint, the self-discipline, the people would have imposed on themselves. It is always easier for the government not to govern, to take the privilege of office without the corresponding responsibility. The rationalization for a failure to exercise leadership can always be placed at the door of the foreign banks. Moreover, government can show that it is trying by compelling the kind of nationa ization that comes with changes in employment practices or public statements by foreign banks of their willingness to allow nationals "participation." Yet, neither tack meets the essential problems of planning for the nation's future.

Nor will these problems be met by the commercial banks. To even attempt to do so would place them in an impossible situation. To deny consumer loans might bring the wrath of consumers that could sharpen into political protest; moreover, it would force the bank from a profitable undertaking in the absence of expressed public policy. And, it is profit, not the bank's individual view of corporate conscience, that is the prime corporate motivator. To deny consumer loans and begin major economic enterprises that may not be fully justified from a business point of view would also constitute a clear invasion of government prerogative, for the banks would not be acting as businesses but as governments.

To say that the people have not evidenced a zeal for self-discipline and that government has not attempted to create that zeal does not end the matter. In varying degrees in each of the island nations there are pockets of opinion that either are, or border on being, revolutionary. With few exceptions bankers have pointed to "the source" of that opinion, the regional University of the West Indies—which has received millions of Canadian dollars from the Canadian government in the form of direct grants.

The university campus is spread among the three more powerful nations: Jamaica, Barbados, and Trinidad and Tobago. Bankers and businessmen have noted that in both Jamaica and Trinidad, governmen in the very recent past has felt compelled to cordon off the campuses because of violent political disturbances. Indeed, in Jamaica, it seems almost as a security matter, a road was built around the campus allowing the university to be sealed off quickly. In Trinidad, the press reported that students were involved in the recent coup d'etat attempt. "We don't pay any attention to them," said a highly placed Trinidadian official. "They do not have any power. We do. Why should the outside world pay attention to them?" To define what "they" want is no easy task. Our concern is not to prove quantitatively the depth and breadth of intellectual revolution, or, for that matter, to describe with specificity the numerous points of discontent. Our purpose is only to emphasize that there are articulated radical views, far more extreme than that of any government. At times, as in the Bahamas, these views find expression in extremist newspapers such as the Bahamian Torch. For many in the Bahamas, good corporate citizenship may be an anomaly; that is, there may be no room for the foreign corporation and for the expatriate employee. Nor may there be room for "degrading" industries such as tourism.

There are those in the Bahamas, to use an extreme example, who would just as soon see the hotels close and the foreign banks with their expatriate employees leave. They would have government direct itself to exploiting the nation's natural resources. Aside from fish, they fail to identify the nature of those resources. Indeed, most analyses of the Bahamas indicate that there are no significant resources aside from its favorable weather and beaches. Even agricultural production to meet the needs of its 200,000 inhabitants is unlikely, for the topsoil is too marginal. Yet, in a sense, it is the expression of such views that allows the government to stay within the scale of political validity when its Finance Minister declares: "Rather than be dictated to by the banks, I would have this island returned to the economy of a fishing village."

As there is a radical left, there is a radical right. In March 1972, the Bahamian government announced a Green Paper on Independence from Great Britain. The government was earlier informed that residents on the island of Abaco, a part of the Bahamas, might secede if independence were obtained. In the view of what might be called the rebel right, England offers stability and growth and saves the Bahamas the expense of managing external affairs. Pressed for more specifics, for a bill of particulars, some of the Abaco residents express both fear and hope. They fear the left as a radicalizing force. They hope to capture what the radical left seems so determined to destroy, namely, tourism and the financial industry. Why, they ask, couldn't Abaco become another Cayman Island? It is well located; its beaches are superior; its population will not insult but rather welcome the North American tourist.

"Who is there to stop us from leaving the Bahamas?" one insurgent asked. "There is no military in the Bahamas. The English are not anxious to become overly involved with either existing or former colonies. The Bahamian government has only four motor police launches. . . . What price would we have to pay for taking up arms against the government?"

The English Parliament granted the Bahamas independence in July 1973, at which time the island of Abaco asked that it remain a colony of Great Britain. That was denied. It remains to be seen whether Abaco will induce internal strain within the Bahamian nation.

THE "INFORMAL" STATEMENT:
UNOFFICIAL ATTITUDES

There would be difficulty enough if the articulated goals of the formal statement were the sum total to be considered here. But there is the other and deeper level of sensitivity which, for our purposes, we have placed under the heading "informal statement." It has a very real bearing on how the articulated goals should be read. In a sense, it is the content of the informal statement that goes to form the emotional base for nationalism, and it is from this base that demands come for "investment dollars with a conscience" and "good corporate citizenship."

Because it is emotion rather than reason that shapes this informa statement, rationality in the context of a nexus between means and goal will not be relevant. Our concern is to describe and understand. In this regard, quantitative data is lacking. The emotional content of nationalism surfaces in no clear demonstrable outline but rather as points from which lines of inference are drawn.

Racism and Tourism

"We are not about to turn our people into a nation of waiters and busboys," said the Deputy Premier and Finance Minister of Grenada. Tourism was to be developed slowly, and whatever else the island has as an economic base was not to be abandoned even if tourism meant considerable material well-being for the people.

The attitude of Grenada is in contrast to that of Jamaica. There the Governor of the Bank of Jamaica and his advisors spoke of tourism as a business that would bring dollars to the island economy. The term "busboys and waiters" with its connotation of economic serfdom was not considered to be applicable. Yet, despite their words of objectivity, there was little doubt that tourism bringing the wealthy white North American did have some influence in government planning. Jamaica with its size and deeper economic base could be more discreet. The tourist dollar was to be sought, but the tourist was to be segregated from the island population. Montego Bay, where the airbound tourist generally is taken, is removed from the population base. And around the port of Kingston where the cruise ships dock, a square-block section of shops and boutiques will be built. The cruise passenger presumably will disembark, walk the square of shops, spend his money, and return to his ship with only minimal person-to-person contact.

Development of small hotels, or pensions, is formal policy for most of the island nations. But capital is not going into it in any significant measure and loan money is not coming from the banks. The risk is too great. Government is offering limited low-interest loans, but for small hotels of 10 to 25 units the white tourist is not the sought-after guest. Rather, the pension tends to be geared towards the black middle-class, either of the nation-state or of North America. The formal words relating to this development are never expressed by government in terms of race. Indeed, in Jamaica the national credo—referring to the island's multiracial composition—is "from many into one." The formal words tend to be expressed as in the statement by the Finance Minister of the Bahamas: "We want to encourage our own people to use the nation's hotels and to travel among the islands."

There is no doubt that racism exists even though a portion of its roots may be in the disparity of wealth between the tourists and the citizens of the host country. The fact is that the tourists generally are white and the citizens generally are black. It is not without reason that several island nations have felt compelled in recent years to launch "courtesy" campaigns, to "educate" their citizens to the need for tourist courtesy. Nor is it without reason that several island airports have parapolice units called "courtesy" forces as a buffer between tourists and citizens.

With an emerging middle class coming largely from the civil service, popular anger can find a feeding source. In Jamaica, as on other islands, government itself has funded some major hotel development and then let management contracts to major hotel chains. Not many years ago, even though a hotel might be owned by the government, blacks often were neither accepted as guests nor served. Indeed, except for menial posts, white expatriates were employed. Not only were the hotels managements white, but so were the lifeguards and housekeepers.

On most islands the situation has changed dramatically. The white employee, except for the manager, accountant, and chef, is no longer present. But the blacks have not forgotten. What makes the situation somewhat more sensitive for the banks is the level of commercial loans to the tourist industry. That is, the banks in their business-loan function often provide short, interim, and more recently, even long-term hotel financing. The loan moneys are the deposits of the citizenry. Native groups often are providing the bulk of moneys used to build and fund enterprises owned and managed by white expatriates. The profits derived from these enterprises then can flow back to the expatriate's nation.

Considering the emotional content of racism and tourism, the commercial foreign banks can be easily viewed not as developers of an economy but as exploiters. They can be characterized as parasites growing fat on the money of the people. From the vantage point of the banks, they are simply making bank-worthy loans that are safe and that will bring a measure of fair return.

Government's response to bank-loan policy has varied. At times, the government (as in Trinidad) requires the bank to obtain a ratio of loan to capital. That is, the hotel entrepreneur must bring a given percentage of his own money in order to borrow local money. At other times the government (as in Antigua) will ask for participation, for a portion of ownership, as a condition to the grant of loan.

Neither measure—ratio of loan to capital or participation—has been brought to public attention. The reasons for this are many: The intricacies of finance are difficult to communicate. The terms of participation might expose individual members of government to charges of conflicts of interest, of "selling out." The terms of participation, even though fair, might exacerbate nationalism.

Racism and Employment

Bank officials will say, "We have always employed natives." And so they have. But until the 1960s those employed were mostly white. Moreover, it was not difficult to find managers who would say, "You must remember these people [the native population] are really quite primitive. It wasn't too many years ago that they came down from the trees."

In the 1960s, matters changed. Few whites were in evidence behind any bank counter. Moreover, most sub-branch managers are now black. Whatever senior white bank officials may feel, the fact remains that basic bank policy has changed to reflect practical business necessities.

Of significance now is the newly found power of government. In the context of past discrimination by whites, how is that power exercised? Does racism play a role? Jamaica can say "from many into one," but one must look hard to find any whites at all in positions of major responsibility in the office of the Governor of the Bank of Jamaica. In Trinidad and Tobago, a substantial portion of the population is of East Indian origin. They constitute an identifiable community. And, what is more important, they are highly skilled businessmen. Yet the heads of the nation's central bank, The Workers' Bank, and the National Commercial Bank are both black. Only their assistants are East Indian. A former member of the East Indian opposition party said, "When this nation sought independence we were promised that we would live together as one. . . . Black nationalism is today a fact of life."

Government is sovereign; it alone holds political control over the banking business. It may be more than lack of understanding and narrow vision that impels government to a restrictive work permit policy. What may be at play is black nationalism. "The minister in charge of work permits," said a Canadian banker, "left no doubt about his feelings. He is a black nationalist. Positions will either be filled by the blacks of this island or not at all. . . . He has gone a long way toward destroying the very business that provides the livelihood of an awful lot of islanders."

Inefficiency and Corruption

Sound economic planning can only take place if there is a will to do it. First with subtle hints, then later more openly, Canadian bankers spoke of inefficiency and corruption within government. To some extent, the inefficiency bears a relationship to racism. Government, on the whole, is unwilling to allow the bankers into their confidence in the making of policy. "Tell me," angrily demanded the Governor of the Bank of Jamaica, "of one government in the world that shares policy-making with the banks it is supposed to control. . . . We set policy and the banks are to follow."

One side of reality is, however, that qualified manpower is all too limited for government to do its job efficiently. And inefficiency is a breeding ground for corruption. On more than one island bankers alluded to bribes paid (though not necessarily by them) for work permits. In Trinidad a banker told of a contractor client whose construction loan was due. The building was completed but the contractor would not be paid until necessary government documents, including an architect's certificate, were obtained. The contractor in a matter-of-fact manner asked for a loan of a few thousand dollars for a few hours. It was granted. He returned at the end of the designated time having "paid" for the government receipts, and in a position to pay the loan.

Corruption at the level described is in itself not cause for great concern. What does trouble some in the banking community, however, is the possibility of a link between nationalism and corruption. That is, can politicians riding the strong wave of nationalism use that force to further their own personal ends? Is it possible for the banking community to become the scapegoat for schemes that are corrupt and that fail?

At issue are not only major economic undertakings but a matter of relationship, and, most important to the banking community, their reputation for financial integrity. Take the airline industry which the more powerful island nations established as a focal point of pride. One of the larger Caribbean carriers is BWIA, largely controlled by the government of Trinidad and Tobago. Since its

establishment several years ago the government has yet to offer an
accounting to Parliament. When a new issue for BWIA was sold to
the public the government itself had to guarantee the issue. What was
speculated about in Trinidad became more clear in the Bahamas.
Government officials and ministers of the state allowed one airline
to fail and then acquired share positions in a new flagship airline,
Flamingo. Whether this action should be judged simple conflict of
interest or corruption is left to the reader.

After reciting the facts concerning Flamingo, a Canadian banker
in the Bahamas turned to a "more serious matter," the possible
entrance of organized crime. The banker pointed to the recent collapse
of a banking house. There was no reason for the collapse. The government had been warned both generally and specifically of the individuals
behind the bank, their reputation, their credit status, and their past
business ventures. The government knew what the facts were, said
the banker. It could have prevented the collapse. The banker drew
the inference that organized crime was making its entrance on the
island. He said that the reputable and established banking community
had the capacity for identifying those bent on looting and for spotting
the use of "hot" money, but that the government would not listen. It
won't listen, the banker said, because it is involved in the corruption.

The banker then pointed to the nation's two gaming casinos, one
on Freeport, the other on Paradise Island in Nassau. Until 1972 both
casinos operated under private enterprise but with government license.
Recently, however, the government made it clear that both casinos
would come under direct government supervision. That is, in the
future the government itself would be operating the casinos. Yet, the
banker said, one of the most important functions of a casino operator
is control, to prevent "skimming." Having in essence decided to
nationalize the casinos, where will the government find the men and
how will it establish the infrastructure to insure control? Indeed,
why in the first instance did the government move toward nationalization? More than one banker pointed to the likelihood of government
involvement with organized crime.

More than one banker also indicated that despite the opportunity
for profit they will not indefinitely accept an erosion of the conditions
necessary to maintain their integrity. After all, money, particularly
international money, can be shifted from one nation to another with
relative ease.

Canadian Values in a Caribbean Setting

Canadian banks, like other foreign banks, do not have a low
physical profile. In the Commonwealth Caribbean they are quite

distinct. In the downtown area they have the same blocklike gloss or heavy stone structure that one would find in North America. It doesn't matter whether one is in the tiny island of Grenada or in the larger areas of Jamaica or Trinidad. Beyond the downtown area are the shopping centers and hotels; in both there are the carbon-copy North American branch banks.

Inside the banks are employees who, except for the fact that they are black, look and dress like their North American counterparts. Their functions are precisely the same as in North America. In the Caribbean as in North America the Bank of Nova Scotia wants to carry the image of the friend to "the man on the street." It wants to do this through its highly developed consumer loan program, the Scotia Plan. It is with some pride that Scotia bankers in the Caribbean and Toronto speak of applying the standards of Toronto in making consumer loans in the Caribbean. The only difference is in the amount to be loaned and the security required. As global corporations operating in the Caribbean, the Canadian banks have transposed much of their Canadian experience south. With that experience have come values, and primary among these values is not to seek out what makes the Caribbean different from but rather what makes it similar to Canada. After all, the Commonwealth Caribbean is not the most important segment of the banks' business. It is only an area where they do business and happen to be dominant. Differences can only be developed where economies of scale allow.

Yet, it is not only the carrying forward of another copy of their Canadian operations and the moneys saved that motivates the banks towards similar behavior. Many of the banks are located so as to serve the North American tourist. In Kingston, Port-of-Spain, or Nassau the downtown banks lie directly in the path that the cruise passenger takes on his walk through town, and in the hotels and shopping centers near fashionable condominiums, it is the tourist and his foreign exchange business that the banks will handle. The thought seems to be that the tourist will feel more comfortable by being placed back again in the bank he left at home.

The native Caribbeans employed by the bank are compelled to become part of the North American environment. As employees their functions and manners are to mirror those of North American employees. Toward these ends, it does not seem improper for the banks to administer North American qualification tests. Nor does it seem improper for bank managers to complain. "It often takes two or more natives to do the job of one Canadian. . . . But we must be patient."

Though the banks are physically located on his island, the Caribbean citizen is asked to perform in an alien setting. He is treated in a removed, objective manner. At the time of employment he seldom is seen by the manager; it is often the accountant who hires him. He is given tests similar to those given in North America, and he often does not do well.

There must be incentive for the Canadian banks to take a different tack. And incentive in the final analysis takes a dollar or profit measurement. The trust companies of the Bahamas are willing to grant senior employees an afternoon off each week to study and take lectures for a qualifying correspondence course given by the Canadian Bankers Association. And the trust company officers will note sadly that, despite the many months since the program's inception, not a single native employee has passed the first part of the multipart qualifying test.

To do more—to devise, administer, and implement special tests, training, and on-the-job programs—would call upon resources the banks may not be willing to commit. At most, the banks could bring nationals slowly to the fore as branch and regional managers and hope that as individuals they would have the capacity to reach other individual employees. But in saying this, it should be understood that the banks have no intention of yielding in matters concerning the way business is to be done. They are working with proud experience. To them banking is banking anywhere in the world. Accordingly, there is little reason why all banks should not look and operate alike.

The Canadian Banker as a Person, a Manifestation of Power, or a Sign of Imperialism

On the larger and more established islands the managing banker is a Canadian expatriate. By North American standards he lives well. By Caribbean standards he often lives on a par with the head of state. His home is owned by the bank and is listed in the telephone as the "manager's residence." Usually the home is in a luxury residential area. It is spacious and staffed by housekeeper and gardeners who are native.

The manager's car on the larger islands is new, long, American, and air-conditioned. At times it is chauffeur-driven. The manager's children usually attend private school, often outside the country. He holds a membership in a country club and, frequently, a separate luncheon club. His material position is impressive. Yet, and this must be emphasized, in the context of the global corporation itself, in the setting of a corporate infrastructure, the managers of the Caribbean would at best be in a middle management position. The assets under their control are often of the same magnitude as those administered by a manager of a single large branch in Toronto or Montreal. The kinds of loans made are restricted in amount and nature and, in any event, subject to ongoing supervision.

Seen in a North American context there is some disparity between the status of the Caribbean manager and his responsibilities. Surely it is not merely a matter of the headquarter banks not knowing or caring. Perhaps it is related to the difficulty of attracting Canadian personnel to the Caribbean. (More than one manager seemed anxious to give up the life he had and return to Canada.) Perhaps, too, the banks were left with no choice. There is usually no clearly marked middle income or upper middle income society into which the manager might move. The more typical situation is the existence of separate areas for the rich, the poor, the tourist, and the retired community.

Whatever the rationale for the status given Caribbean bankers, the fact remains that it is there. Canadian bankers may speak of the need to keep a "low profile" in the Caribbean, but the manner in which they live, their establishment, is "high profile." The rich are visible. A chauffeur-driven car is seen. An expensive walled or fenced home is also seen and is listed in the telephone directory not as that of Mr. _____ but rather as that of the Bank of _____'s manager's house.

By contrast it is interesting to note Trinidad, which was the scene of disorders directed against Canadian banks. It later was shocked by a revolution that nearly succeeded, only to be followed by martial law. The government is faced with increased demand for more material well-being. People are leaving the country, flocking to the city, hoping to share in the relatively high-paying but limited employment pool of the oil industry.

In Trinidad the rich are very sensitive about their status. The head of the Roman Catholic Church has his residence next to that of Trinidad's Prime Minister. It was announced that the Church would vacate the residence; it was too opulent in a nation where there is significant poverty.

It is not suggested that manager's residences be sold and the managers asked to live in poverty. The purpose of this particular comment has been only to note that saying little publicly does not mean that Canadian banks keep a low profile. In areas of poverty, relative wealth is obvious—and it must be assumed that wealth means power.

From the Caribbean point of view, the power of Canadian banks comes largely from the people themselves; it is the money of the people that makes up the bank's assets—and that pays or manager's residence, car, chauffeur, country club, housekeeper, and gardener. The reverse point is made by Donald Fleming, General Manager of the Nova Scotia Trust Company in the Bahamas. Fleming emphasized the number of people, such as housekeepers and gardeners, that are supported through the trust company's operations. He was quite correct in laying claim to such support in that trust company funds are not derived from Bahamians; they come from outside the country. On the other hand, the same cannot be said of commercial banks; their deposit money comes from the residents of the island. It would be a mistake, however, to lay undue stress on just who pays for the signs of material well-being. Stress should be laid on the symbolic power of that status.

The People's View of the Banks

Both bankers and government spoke freely about what they thought the people wanted. But, again, their remarks, while important, had to be taken with a measure of restraint. Each had a point of view, an area of what might be called vested interest. The most useful source for purposes of this study came from newspapers, and from interviews with newspaper editors and reporters. What emerged was no definite profile but rather a random sensitivity to the banking industry. In the small tabloids published in each nation-state there appeared no single sophisticated financial journalist. Matters were seen in simplistic terms: The banks hold money; both the people and the government need money; as good corporate citizens, banks should be responsive to those needs; but, as a condition of that responsiveness, it is only fair for government to be honest and fully disclose its revenue and its expenditures.

Such was the rationale among the more conservative papers. The more radical took more extreme positions: The money of the banks is that of the people; make the loans the people need or face nationalization.

Nowhere could specific banking policy be found to which the majority of people on any one island subscribe. Indeed, the people, the populus, though few in number, clearly had diverse interests. The civil servant wanting a new home or a new car stood in an entirely different position from the individual seeking capital to establish a business. The intellectual at the University of the West Indies stood removed from both the civil servant and the small businessman. The intellectual often was in quest of self-identity. He resented foreign enterprise, and especially foreign banks that used native money to fund foreign enterprise. The intellectual was ready to let his region's economy fall back to the status of a fishing village if to do so would bring popular control over the region's destiny.

Yet neither the civil servant, the small businessman, nor the intellectual, nor all three, constitutes the majority of the area's population. What the majority think remains a puzzle. More significantly, the kind of action they are willing to take based on their beliefs remains a puzzle. There are, however, some points that may go to demonstrate the shape of majority feeling. At the time of national independence nearly all the political parties promised the people not merely a growing economy but riches that would flow from that independence. Even now as the Bahamas, weighed down by major financial troubles, possessed of domestic independence, enters its separate-nation status in its external affairs, a new promise has been given to the people: The external independence will bring an inflow of capital to the island, which the people will control.

A foreign banker in the Bahamas mused: "I remember when domestic independence came to this nation. Their leaders promised heaven on earth. . . . People could be seen and heard passing the large houses of foreigners saying, 'when we get our freedom this will be mine, and that will be mine.'"

The expectations at one time were great. How much reality has taught is another matter. In the Bahamas, the government seems to be acting as if there were no lesson to be learned other than that popular expectations, left unfulfilled once, can be aroused again.

The promises attending nationhood are one matter. Popular feeling toward the foreign commercial banks is another. Everywhere in the Commonwealth Caribbean, save in the most sophisticated urban areas, it is patent that not only are the banks used by much of the population, a great deal of pride is attached to the checkbook and the savings account. It is more than a badge of credit; it is a mark of status. It matters that one is a client of the Bank of Nova Scotia. The bank discovered this when it attempted the first public offering of its securities in Jamaica. The auction market was not sufficiently deep to handle the issue, and the bank's representatives found themselves going to the people to sell shares. They visited the school-houses and through children reached parents who bought a few shares with their savings. A popular stake was acquired in the bank. The "people shares," if such they may be called, are not traded; they are kept under lock in the expectation that the share worth will grow.

The Bank of Nova Scotia demonstrated that with patience and persistence people can be reached. This bank, along with others, fully understands that its services are used by a majority of the people and that the rationale for such use transcends financial need.

It would be erroneous to view the mass of people as objects to be moved by politicians, intellectuals, or petite bourgeoisie. A new branch bank was established in a Trinidad working-class area. Most of the residents used the bank's other facilities; and it was expected that the residents would be all the more willing to use the branch. But in a whisper campaign the branch was boycotted. The reason? No blacks were employed. The main office soon received the meaning of the boycott, blacks were employed, and the residents began doing the expected business with the branch.

CONCLUSIONS

We have not set forth differing viewpoints with the aim of placing blame for existing tensions in the Caribbean. Our concern has been merely to catalogue and describe experience based largely on the interviews that were conducted in Canada and in the Commonwealth Caribbean. The government representatives of the Commonwealth Caribbean were cautious and conservative whether they were heads of state, central bankers, or senior agency officials. On balance, they reflected confidence in a future based upon the past. Only when the questioning became pointed and specific did government representatives begin to discuss the issues and the tensions relating to their nation-states and the banks. This caution was not as evident either with the bankers or the students interviewed, who generally went directly to the perceived problems.

What emerged from the interviews was an understanding that "good corporate citizenship" is not a simplistic concept, and that within each of the interest groups there are motivating factors valid for that group. Thus, government is concerned with national development in the context of sovereignty. The banks are concerned with productivity, with profit. The people, more often than not, are concerned with their own well-being. These objective interests can at times conflict one with the other. Nationalism can conflict with regionalism. Short-term interests can conflict with long-term interests. More particularly, the development of a country may conflict with the profit of a bank. And, personal well-being on a short-term basis may conflict with personal well-being on a long-term basis.

Upon these conflicts must be imposed still another conflict, namely, rationalism against irrationalism. Some may call the conflict by another name. They may refer to it as the conflict between objective and emotional goals. For our purposes, however, it is enough to say that out of the experiences of various groups in and of the Commonwealth Caribbean, sets of values emerge, sometimes not fully articulated, like black nationalism, that can influence decisions. Policies of governments and banks, however rationally based, should bear in mind the potential of these emotional sets.

6

The Canadian banks and the Canadian government share a common interest in the development of the Commonwealth Caribbean. Thus far much has been said of the role of Canadian banks. Their interest in the Commonwealth Caribbean is deep, and they began to sink roots in the area long before the Canadian government became involved in foreign aid or designated the Commonwealth Caribbean as an area of special Canadian concern. In this chapter we will be concerned with the nature and extent of Canadian foreign aid to the Commonwealth Caribbean, and with the question of whether the Canadian banks might not be integrated into new aid schemes.

CONSTRAINTS ON DEVELOPMENT

The Commonwealth Caribbean is a limited land mass surrounded by the warm waters of the Caribbean. It has a growing population. Its governments and people, by and large, have taken to themselves economic progress as a measure of growth. With the lure of indus- trialization, ecology has been assigned lesser priority. In Barbados, for example, a large stack emits black ash next to two of the island's most expensive hotels, one government owned. The stack is part of a Canadian-owned power plant that feeds not only the hotels but, as the Barbadians proudly point out, industry as well. Should mention be made of ecology, a two-pronged reply might be forthcoming: (1) Ecol- ogy is just another way of keeping an island nice for tourists, (2) ecol- ogy is no substitute for jobs and material well-being. The feeling is that the black Commonwealth Caribbean is not to be held down by the white world's view of a "pretty" environment.

Expanding population with limited land and resources is a prob- lem throughout the Caribbean. Barbados, with the most literate population of the Commonwealth Caribbean (98 percent), has perhaps the greatest population density. In 1970 its 241,000 people were living on a total land mass of 166 square miles, a population density of about 1,500 per square mile. This press of people is not about to ease; growth at the rate of about 2 percent annually can be expected and might be accelerated as a result of restricted immigration to the United Kingdom.[1]

In the setting of large population and limited land mass must be added another factor, namely, proximity to affluent North America. It is more than a speculative factor; it is real and pervasive. William G. Demas, a well-known Caribbean economist, wrote in 1965 as head of the Economic Planning Division in Trinidad and Tobago:

> It is interesting to observe one of the absurd aspects of the open economy of the Caribbean. This is the availability of consumer credit (or hire-purchase) facilities for the purchase of imported durable consumer goods. Hire-purchase booms have in more than one case been financed by an inflow of foreign capital. Not only does the system permit the external borrowing to finance consumption; such borrowing is used to finance imports of luxuries or semi-luxuries when there is a large amount of domestic unemployment and when the glaring necessity exists to mobilize domestic resources for development. Needless to say, advertising conspires with the existence of consumer credit facilities to lure people to the delights provided by the gadgets of modern civilization.[2]

Neither a large population nor limited resources have, in sum, dampened popular appetites for the North American way of life. Indeed, the populace, according to Demas, is mortgaging its individual and collective future through borrowing to obtain the consumer goods of North America. For the smaller islands of Grenada, St. Lucia, and Antigua the reality of Demas' point is all too clear in an examination of bank loans (see Tables 3-8). Here loans have exceeded deposits by a considerable margin, and a not inconsiderable portion of such loans have gone directly to consumers or to distributive trades. That is, banks, and this means largely Canadian banks, have on occasion loaned out more than they have taken in by way of deposits. Thus, the money of island people has been used to fund consumer loans and, what is more, the banks have called down additional money from Montreal, Toronto, London, or New York to fund still more consumer purchases.[3]

For Demas, such a situation is absurd. Not only are scarce island savings not being used to build island economies, the island nations are placing themselves still more deeply in debt by importing

TABLE 3

St. Lucia:
Quarterly Analysis of Banks' Loans and Advances
(in thousands)

	Dec. 1967	Dec. 1968	Dec. 1969	March 1970	June 1970
Agriculture	1,972	1,306	564	1,065	1,341
Manufacturing	242	457	239	192	809
Food and nonalcoholic beverages	67	197	44	50	76
Alcoholic beverages	32	—	83	132	86
Clothing and accessories	—	59	—	—	—
Other industries	143	201	112	10	647
Distributive trades	3,481	2,204	3,759	4,058	5,113
Tourism	409	272	635	738	455
Transport	1,337	1,502	1,196	1,152	1,167
Public utilities (gas, telephone, electricity)	573	533	779	400	338
Building and construction	1,305	1,677	2,445	2,361	2,254
Land development and real estate	1,305	1,476			
Personal	1,092	1,243	1,968	2,269	1,966
Other advances	2,680	2,223	3,659	4,072	4,261
Total	14,396	12,893	15,244	16,307	17,704
Long term loans as percentage of total loans	15.7	19.3	23.0	17.1	15.0

	Sept. 1970	Dec. 1970	March 1971	June 1971	Sept. 1971
Agriculture	1,359	1,797	2,030	1,943	4,196
Manufacturing	873	228	449	342	324
Food and nonalcoholic beverages	97	85	125	153	188
Alcoholic beverages	100	39	42	47	45
Clothing and accessories	—	—	—	—	—
Other industries	676	104	282	142	91
Distributive trades	6,008	6,228	6,276	6,526	6,879
Tourism	545	1,750	2,977	2,483	2,344
Transport	1,126	1,001	1,017	1,349	1,407
Public utilities, (gas, telephone, electricity)	406	368	1,538	11,672	1,835
Building and construction	2,434	2,913	3,480	3,462	3,567
Land development and real estate					
Personal	2,672	2,728	2,529	3,243	6,606
Other advances	4,622	4,642	3,432	4,004	4,346
Total	20,045	21,655	23,728	25,024	31,502
Long term loans as percentage of total loans	17.8	17.4	22.3	22.5	29.3

Source: Quarterly Reports of the Eastern Caribbean Currency Authority (Barbados: Research Dept., 1971).

TABLE 4

St. Lucia:
Commercial Banks' Assets
(in thousands)

Period Ending	Cash	Local	Total Abroad	Balances Due by Other Banks				Loans and Advances	Investments	Other Assets	Total Assets
				U.K.	U.S.	Canada	Elsewhere				
1966 December	708	151	4,094	4,077	1	—	16	11,275	—	1,545	17,773
1967 December	721	313	3,914	2,360	47	6	1,501	14,396	—	993	20,337
1968 December	619	203	7,317	1,949	87	1	5,280	12,893	—	1,132	22,164
1969 December	959	191	11,094	10,342	280	90	382	15,244	—	3,072	30,560
1970 December	1,262	313	7,485	3,974	368	84	3,059	21,655	—	2,971	33,686
1971 January	703	341	5,516	3,994	290	66	1,166	23,099	—	2,619	32,278
February	828	236	5,809	4,242	149	98	1,320	22,700	—	2,728	32,301
March	1,061	209	6,670	4,810	81	56	1,723	23,728	—	2,778	34,446
April	712	453	7,896	4,874	168	50	2,804	23,469	—	3,737	36,267
May	967	360	8,299	2,720	124	31	5,424	23,841	—	4,193	37,660
June	1,179	156	7,790	5,736	121	77	1,856	25,024	—	4,822	38,971
July	1,196	1,000	7,741	5,854	—	54	1,833	28,820	250	4,876	43,883
August	1,165	712	7,796	6,413	107	34	1,242	30,114	347	4,312	44,446
September	1,241	601	7,335	6,206	50	67	1,012	31,502	347	3,809	44,835

Source: Quarterly Reports of the Eastern Caribbean Currency Authority (Barbados: Research Dept., 1971).

TABLE 5

Grenada:
Quarterly Analysis of Banks' Loans and Advances
(in thousands)

	Dec. 1968	Dec. 1969	March 1970	June 1970
Agriculture	1,995	2,384	2,325	2,976
Manufacturing	672	1,153	1,137	1,200
Food and Nonalcoholic beverages	233	576	598	387
Alcoholic beverages and tobacco	255	217	193	443
Clothing and accessories	25	75	73	84
Other industries	159	285	273	286
Distributive trades	5,187	7,049	7,166	7,212
Tourism	809	1,188	1,235	1,764
Transport	179	471	496	636
Public utilities (gas, electricity, telephones)	239	59	289	620
Building and construction	756	2,604	3,890	3,674
Land development and real estate	436			
Personal	1,577	2,286	2,459	2,776
Other advances	2,956	5,244	5,047	6,345
Total	14,806	22,438	24,044	27,203
Long-term loans as percentage of total loans	30.4	42.3	39.7	36.1

	Sept. 1970	Dec. 1970	March 1971	June 1971
Agriculture	2,532	2,172	2,448	2,152
Manufacturing	1,449	1,469	1,450	1,760
Food and Nonalcoholic beverages	806	515	649	472
Alcoholic beverages and tobacco	210	415	300	215
Clothing and accessories	138	220	146	163
Other industries	295	319	355	910
Distributive trades	7,928	10,086	10,927	9,239
Tourism	2,276	2,918	3,228	2,724
Transport	828	966	1,219	1,189
Public utilities (gas, electricity, telephones)	1,338	2,078	363	1,012
Building and construction	2,227	2,552	2,154	4,527
Land development and real estate				
Personal	3,212	3,790	4,120	4,252
Other advances	8,950	10,378	10,090	11,766
Total	30,740	36,409	35,999	38,981
Long-term loans as percentage of total loans	36.6	41.3	43.4	36.7

Source: Quarterly Reports of the Eastern Caribbean Currency Authority (Barbados: Research Dept., 1971).

TABLE 6

Grenada:
Commercial Banks' Liabilities
(in thousands)

| Period Ending | Notes in Circulation | Demand Deposits | Time Deposits | Savings Deposits | Total Deposits | Balances Due to Other Banks | | | | | | Other Liabilities | Total Liabilities |
						Local	Total Abroad	U.K.	U.S.	Canada	Elsewhere		
1966 December	1	4,711	6,395	11,746	22,852	434	3,833	–	–	–	–	2,295	29,415
1967 December	1	4,464	6,435	11,694	22,593	477	4,438	–	–	–	–	1,595	29,104
1968 December	1	5,967	9,180	16,569	31,716	383	2,007	211	130	57	1,609	2,981	37,088
1969 December	1	9,752	9,414	20,001	39,167	100	8,969	3,273	93	122	5,481	2,955	51,192
1970 March	1	9,133	8,972	21,424	39,529	113	4,735	2,454	233	339	1,709	2,896	47,274
June	1	7,939	8,605	22,542	39,086	299	5,219	2,916	319	200	1,784	3,041	47,646
September	1	7,637	8,437	23,298	39,372	39	3,285	772	341	96	2,076	6,231	48,928
December	1	6,490	9,236	24,664	40,390	137	2,196	383	344	15	1,454	9,595	52,319
1971 January	1	6,312	9,809	25,066	41,187	168	2,163	374	274	17	1,498	8,776	52,295
February	1	7,204	10,203	24,686	42,093	199	1,878	637	23	15	1,203	9,729	53,900
March	1	7,076	10,187	24,861	42,124	173	1,522	422	71	25	1,004	9,973	53,793
April	1	6,914	10,267	25,199	42,380	386	2,347	74	499	39	1,735	9,625	54,739
May	1	6,807	10,382	25,516	42,705	404	2,467	960	731	7	769	6,254	51,831
June	1	6,327	10,864	25,489	42,680	260	3,003	1,344	896	14	749	6,262	52,206

Source: Quarterly Reports of the Eastern Caribbean Currency Authority (Barbados: Research Dept., 1971).

TABLE 7

Antigua:
Quarterly Analysis of Banks' Loans and Advances
(in thousands)

	Dec. 1967	Dec. 1968	Dec. 1969	March 1970	June 1970
Agriculture	685	644	2,576	1,978	708
Manufacturing	964	14,288	1,887	1,605	4,342
Food and Nonalcoholic beverages	13	196	364	378	374
Alcoholic beverages and tobacco	278	154	37	49	91
Clothing and accessories	102	97	99	104	450
Other industries	571	13,841	1,387	1,074	3,427
Distributive trades	8,367	3,068	3,663	3,608	4,183
Tourism	1,335	956	6,183	6,621	8,013
Transport	629	539	1,195	1,174	1,449
Public utilities (gas, electricity, telephone)	—	—	5	8	102
Building and construction	3,421	629	3,762	4,938	5,041
Land development and real estate	168	439			
Personal	3,545	14.464	14,287	14,786	14,571
Other advances	5,402	5,675	6,846	6,260	5,724
Total	24,516	40,702	40,404	40,978	44,133
Long-term loans as percentage of total loans	31.9	51.7	26.4	43.1	45.9

	Sept. 1970	Dec. 1970	March 1971	June 1971	Sept. 1971
Agriculture	767	676	654	681	705
Manufacturing	4,314	4,963	5,261	5,891	5,438
Food and Nonalcoholic beverages	383	375	379	383	174
Alcoholic beverages and tobacco	78	5	4	6	3
Clothing and accessories	289	236	210	212	192
Other industries	3,564	4,347	4,668	5,218	5,069
Distributive trades	5,723	6,510	6,043	6,071	5,934
Tourism	7,576	7,146	7,569	7,309	7,289
Transport	779	1,504	1,733	2,030	1,789
Public utilities (gas, electricity, telephone)	9	8	115	112	295
Building and construction	4,917	5,540	5,623	5,432	5,471
Land development and real estate					
Personal	14,365	14,101	13,699	14,240	14,345
Other advances	6,177	7,438	6,782	6,970	6,977
Total	44,627	47,886	47,479	48,664	48,243
Long-term loans as percentage of total loans	42.5	40.8	39.0	42.3	45.0

Source: Quarterly Reports of the Eastern Caribbean Currency Authority (Barbados: Research Dept., 1971).

TABLE 8

Antigua: Commercial Banks' Assets
(in thousands)

Period Ending	Cash	Local	Balances Due by Other Banks					Loans and Advances	Investments	Other Assets	Total Assets
			Total Abroad	U.K.	U.S.	Canada	Elsewhere				
1966 December	1,148	416	3,293	2,847	160	170	116	25,315	2,589	1,548	34,309
1967 December	1,249	386	3,800	3,204	265	54	277	24,516	7,269	2,048	39,268
1968 December	1,705	3,667	1,240	-	805	189	246	40,702	6,980	2,988	57,282
1969 December	1,523	798	2,011	408	696	396	511	40,404	6,240	9,817	60,793
1970 December	1,670	719	1,982	72	884	317	709	47,886	5,992	13,204	71,453
1971 January	768	780	3,250	766	408	354	1,722	47,260	6,088	13,204	71,350
February	884	752	1,197	28	802	252	115	47,882	6,084	13,585	70,384
March	979	753	1,334	2	483	164	685	47,479	6,063	14,107	70,715
April	890	960	2,066	65	303	170	1,528	46,694	6,162	13,695	70,467
May	876	764	2,225	30	981	185	1,029	48,152	6,162	13,839	72,018
June	898	534	1,774	-	504	145	1,125	48,664	6,161	13,213	71,244
July	900	945	1,667	8	479	213	967	48,592	6,250	13,206	71,560
August	991	581	1,845	-	612	181	1,052	49,072	6,250	13,369	72,108
September	983	397	2,107	-	533	155	1,419	48,243	6,250	13,287	71,267

Source: Quarterly Reports of the Eastern Caribbean Currency Authority (Barbados: Research Dept., 1971).

money to fund luxury imports. What Demas would have the island nations do is use scarce savings efficiently, and by that he means building a strong economy. But into what business ventures could savings be funneled? For the Commonwealth Caribbean, old answers have merely tended to heighten the economic difficulties posed by Demas. And new answers do not seem particularly well developed or credible. More important, the new answers require a yielding of national sovereignty.

TOURISM: KEY TO DEVELOPMENT?

First, consider one old answer: tourism. All of the Commonwealth Caribbean islands could make tourism a reality. Each is reasonably proximate to the affluent North American market. Each can offer climate, water, and beaches attractive to the North American, even on a year-round basis. Indeed, a 1966 report of what has been called the Tripartite Mission—composed of members of the governments of Canada, the United States, and the United Kingdom and charged with making an economic survey of Barbados and the Leeward and Windward Islands to "formulate plans for the achievement of economic viability and to suggest priorities for the next five years"—found tourism to be the primary solution.[4] Their rationale can be stated simply: Tourism can maximize land use; it can bring in a relatively high revenue per unit of land. Tourism can bring its own capital from abroad; it does not require heavy public infrastructure expenditures. Thus, for the Windward and Leeward Islands only $11.5 million was estimated as needed for 1965-70 to improve air communication, roads to hotels, and promotion.[5] Writing in 1967, Professor Kari Levitt of McGill University and Alister McIntyre of the University of the West Indies in Trinidad commented on the Tripartite Mission:

> The concentration of attention on tourism as the prime growth sector of the islands appears as the fastest way of increasing local income at the least cost in terms of public funds. The Mission does, however, point out the fact that the import content of tourist purchases is high. Thus, an increase in tourist expenditures of $10 million in Antigua was estimated to generate an increase in GDP [Gross Disposal Product] of $8 million; but because of the island's very high propensity to import, it would also give rise to an estimated increase in imports of $10 million. The net effect on the balance of payments would thus be zero. To quote the Mission: "The effectiveness of tourism as a growth generator depends

91

therefore on reducing not only the import content of
tourist expenditure, but of expenditure as a whole in
the islands, since, if almost all the foreign exchange
earned is spent on consumer products, little or no
foreign exchange remains to finance the imports
resulting from investment in infrastructure and social
services." Tourism must be supplemented by a major
effort in import substitution, particularly of food items.[6]

Levitt and McIntyre set out their answer to the problems of tourism:
Let there be better utilization of existing capacity. That is, let the
Caribbean become a year-round resort catering to lower income North
Americans and West Indians. Moreover, as part of this effort, hotels
could feature local island foods. Available public funds could then be
more readily used to revitalize agriculture, encourage interisland
trade, and even later to export food to Canada and the United States.
Finally, it was thought that an appeal directed to lower income groups
and the use of island produce might lessen social tension; islanders
and nonislanders could mix.

Tourist development, in our opinion, should be encouraged to develop within constraints which insure that this
industry does not develop enclaves of North American
privilege in the islands. Thus, care should be taken to
preserve public beach rights, to prevent outright purchase
of smaller islands, to insure that good agricultural land
is not pre-empted for tourist development, and to control
entertainment in order to prevent casino and gambling
activities which are obviously undesirable for social
reasons. In short, the appeal of tourism in terms of its
apparent high yield of income for low expenditure of
public funds should be tempered by an appreciation of
the West Indian view which welcomes foreign tourists
who wish to enjoy the beauty of the tropics and the way
of life of the islands, without imposing their presence
as an alien force.[7]

Soon after the Tripartite Mission report and the comments of
Professors Levitt and McIntyre—whose study was sponsored by the
Canadian Trade Committee, Private Planning Association of Canada,
and the Centre for Developing Area Studies of McGill University—came
another report. Titled "The Future of Tourism in the Eastern Caribbean," it was prepared by H. Zinder and Associates, Inc., of Washington, D.C., under contract with the Agency for International Development
and sponsored by the Regional Development Agency.[8] The report

focused primarily on the islands of Antigua, St. Kitts and Nevis, Montserrat, Dominica, St. Lucia, Barbados, St. Vincent, and Grenada. Section 1 of the Zinder report begins:

> From the view of the tourist, the principal assets of the
> Eastern Caribbean are sun and water. From a technical
> point of view, the principal asset of the region is its
> geographic position. In other words, it is close enough
> to the heavy population centers of North America, so
> that tourists who have been visiting the Northern Carib-
> bean in large numbers are beginning to find their way
> down to the Leeward and Windward islands.

Notice that the report speaks of attraction in terms of place, in terms of sun and water. Nothing is said of people. North Americans do not visit the Caribbean to learn of culture, to meet people. They do not visit the Caribbean for the same reasons they might travel to the ruins of the Mayan civilization. They do not visit the Caribbean for the same reasons that they might fly to the nastiness of a London winter for a vacation. What the Zinder report sets forth in the very first paragraph is the rather brutal fact that most North Americans are either neutral or simply do not want to come into contact with the people of the Caribbean.

Most North Americans probably would be quite content to visit islands in the Caribbean that contained no native people, so long as the amenities of life are afforded. And, indeed, that is precisely what has taken place in many of the island nations. In the Bahamas the major casino-resorts are physically removed either by bridge or distance from the centers of population. In Jamaica the government is planning for the cruise tourist what the air tourist has in Montego Bay, namely, separation from the people. In downtown Kingston, as mentioned earlier, a shopping-tourist-convention center mall will be built which will hug the waterfront, ensuring that the tourist will not need to visit other shops or walk Kingston's streets. So, too, in Trinidad one finds a major tourist hotel perched on a hill removed from the city. Indeed, even in Barbados, known for its relatively friendly and courteous inhabitants, the deluxe hotels have been sited in enclaves; both Barbadian and North American must make some effort to come into contact with each other. Tiny Antigua, like the Bahamas, has one dependency, Barbuda, partly owned by foreigners who operate a full-service hotel; guests need not travel to Antigua for any of their needs.

The separation of land from people is real. It extends to more than the site of a hotel. It extends as well to way of life. In London, or Paris, or Israel, a tourist might try to fit himself into the host country's way of life. More often than not the tourist will not feel discomfited by changes in routine flowing from a visit to London, Paris, or Israel, but rather will feel a sense of reward; the journey will have been worth the price, for something will have been learned of the host people. The same is not true in the Caribbean. Security guards, often in the direct employ of the hotels, keep "strangers" away from hotel premises. In deluxe hotels accommodations are very similar to deluxe accommodations in North America. Commonwealth Holiday Inns, the Canadian counterpart of the large American enterprise, has simply endeavored to transplant its experience and facilities in, for example, Toronto, to St. Lucia, Grenada, Barbados, and Antigua. Not only are the rooms similar, but the menus are very much the same. It is not native fish, poultry, or beef that is offered. Rather, the menus feature Canadian-fed beef imported from the prairie provinces.

To meet felt tourist needs, walls of separation are built. But the walls do not keep out the obvious social tensions. The building of the walls themselves can exacerbate those tensions. The islands are not large, but small. Their populations are not sparse, but substantial. On the whole, the people are not wealthy, but poor. To carve a tourist enclave is to commit an act that an island population must live with daily. For whatever reason the walls are built, their existence must be characterized as a kind of rejection. That rejection cannot be denied its racial overtones, for the fact that most North American tourists are white and most Caribbean inhabitants are black cannot be ignored.

Violence occurs at times. In the U.S. Virgin Islands there is a Rockefeller resort, luxurious and isolated. In September 1972 several tourists stood around an outside bar after a round of golf. Six men burst from a nearby hedge, armed, and wearing military fatigues. They fired at all, killing four Miami residents and four club employees. As reported in Time,

> The gunmen methodically scooped up about $700 from the club's cash registers and casually collected the wallets and purses of the dead and dying. Then they walked away toward the hills, according to a man who watched, "with their guns slung over their shounders as if they were bird hunters." . . . Islanders have grown used to grumbling about a rise in the crime rate and the bands of youths that sometimes wander round nearby Christiansted at night. But they were stunned by what Governor Melvin Evans called "the most heinous crime I can recall." Some tourists wondered whether the real motive for the crime might have been political or racial; all the gunmen were black, apparently, and seven of the eight victims were white. But police believed that the crime was merely a particularly vicious case of armed robbery. At week's end, the police

arrested two men in the case and charged them each with
eight counts of murder.[9]

By August 1973 convictions were obtained. As the guilty left the court-
room they shouted black power slogans. At the same time, several
other murders of whites took place on the islands, and the Governor
sought and obtained a supporting force of U.S. marshals from the main-
land.
Antigua is not far from the Virgin Islands, and until a few years
ago Antiguans could ignore Virgin Island law and obtain relatively high
paying jobs without work permits. But that has changed, perhaps in
part because of unemployment in the Virgin Islands itself. Antiguans
were expelled and sent back to Antigua, where the unemployment picture
is even more bleak. It is not uncommon to see young men sitting in
clusters near the side of the roads simply waiting and looking. Now
add to this a heavy dependency by Antigua on tourism and the bleak
picture begins to take on some dangerous signs. The Zinder report
stated:

> If there were no tourism, the islands' economies would
> sag considerably more than just the amount of money
> directly involved in tourism. The multiplier effects of
> tourist spending would begin to decline, taking with them
> a range of businesses that could not survive without the
> income generated by tourist spending. . . . Of all the
> islands covered in the survey, the contribution to national
> income of tourism is highest in Antigua.[10]

For Antigua the bare figures are dramatic. The Zinder report
estimated that when national income is taken into account and compared
with the impact of tourist spending, Antigua stands first by a significant
margin: About 89 percent is the estimated impact of tourism on national income. For Barbados the impact is 40 percent; St. Lucia 46
percent; and Grenada 40 percent.
From the point of view of government financing there is an obvious
relationship between tourism and national income. Tourism is a source
for tax moneys. In Antigua, Zinder estimates, it provides 78 percent
of all tax revenues. This again contrasts with Barbados, 27 percent;
Grenada, 25 percent; and St. Lucia, 10 percent. An even greater contrast with Antigua is Trinidad and Tobago. There a deeper-layered
economy, natural resources, and a larger population have combined
to minimize the importance of tourism; the impact of tourism on
national income is only 5 percent, and the tourist industry accounts
for only 5 percent of tax revenues.[11]

In a number of respects the Zinder report was heavily critical of Antigua. For our purposes, however, the critique can be generalized: (1) Antigua was not spending enough to promote tourism. (2) Antigua had not created the infrastructure necessary to support either new or existing hotels. The water supply was inadequate, power failures were all too frequent, telephone service was not complete, roads were poor.[12] This phase of the critique was in reality a comment on Antiguan government. It seemed to say that tourism, so critical to the island economy, could evaporate unless government put its house in order and made an environment conducive to the well-being of tourists.

Such an environment extends beyond the physical; it goes beyond good roads and electricity. While the tourist may not particularly care to steep himself in an island's culture, he certainly does not take an expensive vacation to be insulted. Of Antigua, its people, and its government the Zinder report stated:

> Antigua is particularly afflicted with the problem of [hostile] attitudes toward tourists, particularly at places where tourists stay or visit such as hotels, resorts, shops, and the airport. We suggest that the tourist board get together with hoteliers, airport officials, and the unions and see what can be done to improve the situation. Probably this is a matter of training. But it's also a matter of informing workers about the importance and value of tourism, and this suggests an internal "pro-tourism" promotional campaign, introduced gradually, and maintained over a long period of time.[13]

To put it mildly, there is unrest in Antigua. Once a favorite vacation spot for tourists, the island has lost some of its attraction. Morally, perhaps, it would be well to ask: Why should the Antiguans bear full responsibility for change? Why shouldn't the visitors coming in such great numbers and with relatively such great wealth accommodate themselves to the island, its culture, and its people? The answer is simple: The tourist does not have to come to Antigua. He has the money to take him elsewhere, to any one of many islands that will offer seclusion without demanding change or adjustment on his part. In sum, the tourist does not need Antigua, but Antigua needs the tourist.

All this is set out merely to state the matter rationally. Morality in a deeper sense has been put to one side. Having stated the matter rationally, many expect the Antiguan government and its people to respond with reason, with intelligence. That is, they should act in their own self-interest; they should do what is necessary to make the tourist comfortable, or they should move with purpose to develop the economy in some other way.

Yet, three years after the Zinder report, and even with a change in Antiguan government, most observers would have to conclude that the reasoned response has not been forthcoming. Native hostility to tourists persists. What is more, that hostility has carried over to the business sector generally. What must at least be called a vocal minority has invoked the proposition "Antigua for Antiguans." Hotels are to be owned in whole or in part by Antiguans. And the money flow representative of island savings, the commercial banks now in foreign hands, are to be given an Antiguan cast. Indeed, on the wall of one Canadian bank in Antigua can be seen in large painted letters the word "Nationalize." There is a troubled environment in the view not only of hotel operators but, more important perhaps, in the view of the banking community. (Judging from one-to two-hour interviews I conducted in Antigua with the managers of three Canadian banks and one American bank, this appeared to be the prevailing opinion.) That view strikes at what it has characterized as inept government leadership, inept at planning for what must be done for a viable economy, and inept in failing to lead the people away from the kind of hostility which is self-destructive.

Not without reason, some of the smaller islands, viewing Antigua and possibly the Bahamas, have placed less emphasis on tourism. For example, in interviews I conducted in 1971 with the Minister of Finance, Trade, and Production for Grenada, he made it abundantly clear that the government would not allow tourism to become the island's dominant industry. The rationale was simplistic: Government did not want the island people to become a nation of servants.[14] Right or wrong, the feeling was firm. It does no good to argue that it is only a feeling, that people could be trained to a different self-image. That is the image presently held. In a sense what the government of Grenada said reflects the earlier conclusions of the Tripartite Mission, which found that

> ... local opinion, in several smaller islands, was not much in favour of a major development of the tourist industry. The reasons for such reservations on the part of local opinion are surely not difficult to understand if we consider the social consequences of uncontrolled tourism in pre-Castro Cuba, Puerto Rico, the Bahamas, and even on the north coast of Jamaica.[15]

The Zinder report criticized Grenada for building a school on one of the more attractive points of an already lovely island. This was not effective, efficient land use. More money could have been brought to the island by having a hotel located there. In the future, the Zinder report stated, better hotel planning is needed.[16] The report emphasized the importance of the example:

> We single out this particular example because the cliff
> area at Sauteurs has a truly superb view of the most
> southerly of the Grenadines; the place could serve as
> an anchor-point for a round-the-island tour. But now it
> probably can't be unless the church and graveyard were
> removed (a dubious development and not recommended).
> Yet, even if that were done, the school's being right on
> top of the site limits its usefulness for tourism. (Inci-
> dentally, the school reportedly was financed by bilateral
> aid.)[17]

The parenthetical remark draws foreign aid into the picture. Foreign aid has often funded the infrastructure—the airports, the roads, the water and electricity services—needed for tourism. Without the initial heavy capital expenditures needed for an infrastructure, tourism could only be a marginal industry on any island, for the means would not be there to serve and attract great numbers of people. And the basic fact of a lack of capital to provide such funding is true of all the islands, especially the smaller islands that do not have any but a single-line economy, namely, agriculture. Without foreign aid funding the necessary infrastructure, tourism could not exist as an industry.

In 1970 the Canadian Senate Standing Committee on Foreign Affairs conducted hearings on the Caribbean area. While to some extent the hearings emanated from riots in Trinidad and Tobago against Canadian banks, they had a more solid base. They were a further examination of the 1966 Commonwealth Caribbean-Canada Heads of Government Conference.[18] (More will be said of the conference later.) Testimony before the Committee by the Canadian University Service Overseas (CUSO) stated:

> We have noted that you have discussed often the area of
> tourism as an incentive or contributing factor to economic
> growth. We would only like to add a few comments which
> we have received from various West Indian economists
> and politicians. There is no basic disagreement that
> tourism can contribute to economic growth—the question
> which seems more relevant is, whose growth and/or at
> what price—it is a political-sociological consideration
> rather than just an economic one. Many West Indians
> ask "who will reap the benefits?" and "do we want our

country overrun by the sun-sand-sea-sex syndrome citizens of the West." Or as another West Indian put it to us, "There is something very arrogant about Western concepts of tourism—they travel two or three thousand miles to come to our country, but they want to stay in the same kind of hotels they have at home, eat the identical foods they eat at home and have us wait upon them hand and foot. The Western colonial mentality really hasn't changed." These are, of course, extreme views and perhaps overly negative. But the basic question of "what price" economically, socially, culturally and politically will have to be paid, is to many, a crucial concern.[19]

CUSO's testimony must have had some effect. The Senate Committee recognized that the Commonwealth Caribbean is in a state of change, and, in this regard the Committee urged the maintenance of a "perspective" to avoid excessive reaction by the Canadian public. Good mutual relations between nation-states must be maintained. Canada must demonstrate more than a concern with stability; it must recognize the "case for progressive change".[20] So it was that the Committee in part deemphasized the role of tourism. Referring to Canada's aid dispenser, the Canadian International Development Agency, (CIDA), the Committee stated:

The present CIDA policy of special concentration in the smaller islands of the Eastern Caribbean is well-founded. The five-year planning principle in this programme is also a step in the right direction, but the Committee is concerned about too great a reliance on the development of tourism. The programme should remain flexible, and CIDA should respond favourably to requests for increased assistance to the agricultural sector.[21]

Tourism, in summary, can be a complicating rather than an ameliorating factor in the resolution of an island's problems. A flourishing tourist industry may not be a panacea, nor does it always matter that an island's population prospers from tourism. Much depends on self-image. If a population views itself as cleaning persons and servants being degraded by wealthy whites, there is only a limited amount the whites can do to change that self-image. Horace Sutton, in an article in the Saturday Review, describes the attitude of Bobby Hill, a black 27-year-old teacher of African history at Dartmouth:

Like most Caribbean radical leaders, he views tourism in its present form as a degrading evil. He thinks the

Jamaican north coast has been turned into "one large
pimping area." . . . He sees future tourism in the form
of small guest houses—cottage tourism geared for the
black middle-class American.[22]

Sutton points out that the anti-tourism concepts are by no means universal in the area:

Bahamian Prime Minister Pindling sees his economy
based on tourism "for some time to come." And, although
Williams in Trinidad has given lip service to cottage tourism and has held off casinos, he has acceded to a new wing
on the government-owned Hilton and a new Holiday Inn.
Michael Manley in Jamaica, a leader possessed of
enormous political electricity who might well be the next
Jamaican Prime Minister, backs tourism as a labor-
intensive industry and decries those who, as one British
Honduras radical did, equate tourism with whorism.
"I've never seen any Swiss person who seemed particularly whorish to me," he says. "The challenge to Jamaica
is not to be trapped into irrelevances as to what the dividing line is between call girl, wife, mistress, and whore.
They all end up doing the same thing, and there is an economic base to what each of them does. I've never been
able to convince myself that there is a difference in taking
an order from a superior in a dull, monotonous factory
and serving somebody a plate of food."[23]

When native hostility and even hatred of tourists arises it does
so in a context that was stated earlier in this chapter: Zero population growth is not a characteristic of the Commonwealth Caribbean.
Each of the island nations has experienced sustained population growth
that has been only partially offset by emigration. CUSO stated, "With
the population growth, the manpower division estimates 15,000 persons
will have to emigrate each year. The difficulty lies with the selective
quality demanded by developed countries."[24]
A story is told that illustrates the difficulty. A developed nation
experienced a severe shortage of nurses. Recruiters visited Jamaica
and were able to offer the kinds of salaries that induced emigration,
leaving Jamaica with a nurse shortage.[25] More than one senior island
government official stated in interviews: "We don't want to solve our
population problem by exporting needed talent." Yet, should unskilled
labor be permitted to emigrate, major responsibilities are imposed
on the host country. It must aid in the process of effective absorption.
But even a sincere attempt to do so will not obviate all difficulties.

As recently as September 1972 the Toronto Globe and Mail reported:
"West Indian girls who come to Metro [Toronto] and work as domestics are being exploited by low wages and long hours, a committee of
social workers found yesterday."26 Underlying the story was not only
an implication of separate treatment, but racial discrimination. It did
not matter that all domestics share the same lot throughout Canada
in terms of being outside certain statutory protections.

Sustained population growth must affect not only an island's
economy but its value structure. Emigration to a country not fully
prepared to accept those coming will not resolve but rather may com-
plicate relations between nation-states. And just as important is the
basic physical fact of increased population density on limited land.
Housing must become more expensive, more crowded; streets must
become more congested; food produced at the same volume level must
become more expensive.

Now enters the deluxe tourist hotel. It may offer a clean and
spacious beach denied to islanders. It will offer accommodations
that are enormously extravagant by island standards. It will provide
food that cannot be bought by islanders. And the hotels will charge
and the tourist will pay sums that simply have no relationship to a
native's income. CUSO states:

> At the root it seems much of the frustration and increas-
> ing animosity is due to a recognition that despite political
> independence there is no economic independence and per-
> haps therefore, no true political independence. This, of
> course, is not a new thesis. Years ago, Marti speaking
> of Latin America said: "He who speaks of economic
> union speaks of political union. The nation that buys,
> commands and the nation that sells, serves. It is neces-
> sary to balance trade in order to ensure freedom." For
> some West Indians, the Caribbean states are more depend-
> ent now than they were prior to independence. They are
> more dependent on trade, tariffs, barriers and regulations,
> duties and customs restrictions, the G.A.T.T. etc., which
> were designed, in their view, by the "rich and for the
> rich."
>
> At the same time we are all aware there is a grow-
> ing white, or foreign presence in the islands. An expa-
> triate presence, both in business and as tourists, which
> seems to West Indians, extremely affluent, which intensi-
> fies the gap between the indigenous people striving for
> economic survival and those who bathe in affluence—the
> traditional gap—the rich and the poor. This affluence,
> however, this gap, is noticed more by the have nots and,

in many senses, the affluence is addictive. The desire to be as affluent is growing and yet this is not easily obtainable. Hence, some of the frustration.

The radicals, however, very often ask us "why is it that foreign business can be extremely profitable in our own countries and we do not seem to be able to profit as much. Why is it that Alcan, the banks, the insurance companies, Distillers Corporation—Seagrams Ltd., Sheriffs (Jamaica) Ltd., Colgate Palmolive, Brandram-Henderson (CIL) Ltd., Winnwell Manufacturing Co. (leather goods), Waterman Leather Products, Bata Shoe, Jamaica Fibre Glass Company, etc. all seem to be very profitable and most West Indians are not ".[27]

Native anger, born of frustration, can spill over to more than the tourist, who, after all, can simply pack his bags and return no more. Native anger can be directed toward Canada's most visible enterprise, namely, its banks. On any one island, even the smallest, one finds not just a single Canadian bank, but many, and each of them more often than not has branches. The bank is the primary mechanism for money flow. The people use it to deposit their savings which, in turn, are loaned out on a short-term basis, often for consumer loans. Government is compelled to use the banks for financing portions of the nation's debts and for assistance in the control of currency. The banks, in sum, might be likened to the very important retail establishments in a ghetto. They handle the commodity that allows for material well-being. They make profits from the effective use of other people's moneys. And, apparently, they make a rather substantial profit at that. The white expatriate manager on each island has his own home, usually the best the island can offer. Can there be any doubt that the banks of Canada in time of civil unrest stand in an exposed position? The prestigious Canadian Annual Review for 1970, referring in part to the student destruction of the $1 million Computer Centre of Sir George Williams University, Montreal, in which West Indians were implicated, put the matter well:

Canada an imperialist nation? Canada a nation that controls the financial affairs of a small neighbour? Canada a racist state that discriminates against blacks? This appears to be the reaction of large elements of the population in Port of Spain, Trinidad, when a series of riots and demonstrations, complete with vandalism against Canadian companies' property, took place in early March. The cause was the trial of ten West Indian students on charges developing

from the "computer centre party" at Montreal's
Sir George Williams University. The deeper cause,
it seemed, was a response to the low wages paid by
Canadian concerns in the Caribbean, the control of
the banking and insurance system by Canadian firms,
and concern about governmental trade practices.[28]

The deeper cause referred to by the Canadian Annual Review has
not been fully resolved. Donald Fleming, Q.C., a former Minister of
Finance of Canada, now Managing Director of the Bank of Nova Scotia
Trust Company (Bahamas) Ltd., spoke in 1972 of the damage flowing
from the Trinidad riots attendant to the trial of the ten West Indian
students:

> The insurrection last spring in Trinidad, mob violence
> there and in other countries, and policies of nationali-
> zation of resource industries, banks and other financial
> institutions have seriously damaged the entire [Common-
> wealth Caribbean] area, including the country, in the eyes
> of investors abroad.[29]

The damage Mr. Fleming spoke of related to damage of investor confidence that spilled over and affected banking activity. It was damage
that could only be repaired by restoration of government credibility,
and this necessitated a willingness on the part of government to have
a "dialogue" with the banks, to discuss problems and plans.

A few months after the speech of the former Minister of Finance,
a column appeared on the front page of the business section of a Bahamian paper. Titled, "Attention Mr. Banker Sir!", it mentioned the
call for dialogue. But it did not speak words of conciliation. Rather,
it spoke of the need for bankers to serve Bahamian small business.
Once this was done then there might be "dialogue" with government.
The column is set out with some detail, for its angry tone is worth
grasping:

> However, Mr. Local Banker, you may, sir, not concede
> that a gap exists between yourself and the Bahamian
> businessman. If you do, sir, kindly allow me to ask
> you to keep your ear to the ground. For many business-
> men are saying, sir, very mean things about you and your
> lending habits.
>
> Many say sir, for example, that you practice
> racial discrimination in your lending practices.
>
> Many say, sir, that you refuse to have confidence
> in Bahamians when the sums involved become really
> material (say, for example, in the six or seven figures).

Many say, sir, that all you want to lend money for
is things like cars.

Many say, sir, that even if you are prepared to
lend a businessman one nickel you demand his life as
security.

Many say, sir, that you seem to have little authority
here and have to run to head office overseas to find direc-
tions for everything sir.

Many say, sir, that you are not helpful in the ways
that bankers in the more developed countries are reputed
to be.

Many say, sir, that you refuse to Bahamianize your
personal attitudes despite constant requests from the
Government leaders, sir.

Many say, in short, that you, sir, have no compas-
sion, social conscience or appreciation for the problems
of small businessmen in a developing country, which
happens to have a racial composition like the Bahamas.

Whether or not all of these charges are true,
Mr. Banker, you stand accused. A charged man, under
our system of justice sir, must give a plea. In this case,
sir, the magistrate is your client and potential client.
Whatever your plea is, sir, kindly let the magistrate
know in no uncertain terms.[30]

No amount of foreign aid by the Canadian government can eliminate all major problems in the Commonwealth Caribbean. Yet the
nature of the Canadian presence is such that action or nonaction by
the Canadian government could trigger a response affecting Canada's
most important global corporations, its banks. The trial of West
Indian students at Sir George Williams did result in an attack on
Canadian banks in Trinidad. The same students might well have been
brought to Canada as a form of assistance. Indeed, immigration to
Canada from the Commonwealth Caribbean has been at the rate of
14,000 a year, another sign of Canada's special relationship, and, as
such, indicative of special problems. Let there be no doubt that claims
of discrimination against West Indians in Toronto will not touch the
white bankers of Canada in Trinidad, Jamaica, Antigua, or the Bahamas.

Where a nation's own economic interests are involved, where
its prestige is at stake, the consistent pursuit of principle in the
formulation of aid policy can sometimes be difficult. On the face of
it, Canada may favor "progressive" government programs in the
Commonwealth Caribbean, but Canada would be hard pressed to give
a blanket seal of approval to the nationalization of its banks in the
same area.

A series of constraints operate upon Canada that make the formulation of an effective aid program difficult. It is this rather simplistic proposition that has been the thrust of this section on tourism. No single aid approach will suffice. Building deluxe hotels in large numbers will not at this time resolve the difficulties of the Commonwealth Caribbean. Indeed, tourism, often held as the primary solution, may well exacerbate social and economic problems. Any aid program must consider elementary facts: Island population is large and growing, land is scarce, density is great. And in this setting, Canadian banks have substantial influence over native savings which could form a part of any developmental scheme. But these moneys have been used largely to feed consumer appetites developed in part because of contact with tourists and proximity to affluent North America. Indeed, as Mr. Demas earlier noted, money has even been imported at quite profitable rates to allow consumers to borrow to buy imported goods.

REGIONALISM: ANOTHER APPROACH TO DEVELOPMENT

Economists have pointed to a solution, namely, "rationalization." Translated into action, this calls for regional economic institutions. Island nations must pool resources; they must act in concert. Professors Levitt and McIntyre have written:

> Because of the limited size of the markets of the individual territories, integration is a sine qua non of further successful industrialization in the Caribbean. It is also more than this. It offers the region an opportunity to develop an aluminum complex using the bauxite resources of both Jamaica and Guyana and the hydro-electric power of Guyana. . . . It may also help to create an assured market for the development of a petro-chemical complex in Trinidad and Tobago. The recent expression of interest in aluminum production in Guyana by the Aluminum Company of Canada is a most enlightened step. The active cooperation of Alcan with Caribbean governments in the development of an aluminum complex extending perhaps even to the manufacture of a few suitable final products, such as siding for house construction in the Commonwealth Caribbean, could be one of Canada's most decisive and enlightened contributions to the economic progress of the area.[31]

Integration, the existence of a free trade area, would also have to take cognizance of what Canada would call "regional disparity."

That is, some areas of the Caribbean are more fully developed than others. To avoid "polarization," a drift of population and power to a few nations such as Jamaica, Trinidad and Tobago, and Barbados, a balance would have to be struck. Specifically, the smaller nation-states must be given stimuli for agricultural exports and small industry. In short, the larger islands could, by way of example, import foodstuffs that could be grown and processed on some of the smaller islands.32

Economists such as Demas and Professors Levitt and McIntyre point to economic integration as a solution. In doing so, they recognize that it is not a full solution. Integration will not totally resolve the economic problems of the Caribbean.

Even if it [the Commonwealth Caribbean] becomes integrated economically, [it] will still be a region that experiences a great deal of external dependence. Even though in an integrated region a slightly less dependent pattern of development might become possible, yet the reliance on overseas markets will still be great. The world market for manufactured goods, with all its hazards and all its opportunities, will still remain to be conquered, and, even when the region rids itself of dependence on external aid, it may still be an important recipient of private capital inflow.33

Integration has its limitations, but at least it may be a start toward fuller development. It would seem that the inducements and compulsions to integration should already have brought the Commonwealth Caribbean to a free market. Some of the inducements have been noted. A few words should be offered touching upon the compulsions. The neighbors of the Commonwealth Caribbean are forming their own trading blocs with the result that the Commonwealth Caribbean is increasingly placed in a position of economic isolation. Latin America has the capacity for economic integration with a population exceeding 240 million and a per capita income of about U.S. $300. In countries such as Mexico and Brazil, industrial development has proceeded quite far. The area is, on the whole, well-endowed with natural resources. Population is expected to reach 400 million by 1985. To the north, the United States is sheltering its own manufacturers, urging them to return or stay through tax incentive programs. Canada is responding in kind. With England's entry into the Common Market, the former Commonwealth protections available to the Commonwealth Caribbean are disintegrating. Couple large-bloc economic integration with Caribbean high population, limited land, and marginal resources. Can there rationally be any alternative to regional development? The

Canadian Senate Committee on Foreign Affairs, studying the Caribbean, recommended

> . . . continuing support of projects and programmes leading to regional cooperation and integration. The present assistance to the University of the West Indies and the Regional Development Bank is highly effective for this purpose. All cooperative projects must proceed, however, at the pace agreed upon by the governments of the area and no regional institution should become too dependent on outside support.[34]

Canada, said the Senate Committee, should be supportive of regionalism. But, and this is most important, Canada should take specific action implementing the principle of regionalism only to the extent that the participating countries so desire. Such a policy would require Canada to seek consensus for any regional program and to abandon its support once that consensus was removed. More particularly, the committee specifically noted that the Commonwealth Caribbean is not homogeneous; it has diversity, and that diversity should be respected. Regional cooperation should be approached with great care.[35]

There is a certain virtue in the approach of the Senate Committee. The practicality of the recommendation may be another matter. Take the two institutions cited in the committee recommendation, namely, the Regional Development Bank and the University of the West Indies. As contrasted to the Caribbean Free Trade Association (Carifta)[36] in which 12 Caribbean nations joined to allow for a free flow of products between them, the Regional or Caribbean Development Bank and the University of the West Indies are heavily funded and were initially staffed by Canada and the United Kingdom.

THE CARIBBEAN DEVELOPMENT BANK: REGIONALISM OR FEDERALISM?

The Caribbean Development Bank is relatively new. It was established by an agreement signed in Kingston, Jamaica, on October 18, 1969, and came into force on January 26, 1970, with headquarters in Barbados. The Bank is to "contribute to the harmonious economic growth and development of the Member countries in the Caribbean . . . and promote economic cooperation and integration among them, having special and urgent regard to the needs of the less developed members of the region."[37]

In many respects the Bank can be viewed as a special lender of last resort. It is a merchant bank that will make loans on potentially profitable undertakings, but only if the funds are not otherwise available from private enterprises. Moreover, the Bank will not loan to member governments if the purpose is merely to help those governments fund a debt. Nor will it loan to private entities if the purpose is to provide working capital. Primarily the Bank is concerned with the potential multiplier effect of the business venture on the economy. The social or cultural impact of those businesses is not, on the face of the Bank's criteria for operations, of great moment.

> The Bank contributes to the financing of public and private
> projects related directly to economic development. In its
> evaluation of the projects it finances, the Bank gives weight
> to their multiplying effect in the general economic activity
> in the country concerned; the extent to which they would
> assist in overcoming obstacles to national development;
> their ability to reduce imports or earn foreign exchange;
> the introduction of new industries or of new techniques to
> raise productivity; the expansion of employment opportu-
> nities; and the contribution of the project to the economic
> cooperation and integration in the area.[38]

The Bank, to repeat, is a merchant enterprise. It does not pro-vide the whole of a loan. It uses its resources to encourage and sup-port capital formation, the coming together of money to fund an under-taking. The social or cultural impact of a project would seem to have meaning for the Bank only to the extent that these might constitute factors hindering economic success.

It was to such an enterprise that Canada subscribed to $10 mil-lion, 20 percent of authorized capital. Canada and the United Kingdom, holding equal positions, became the two nonregional Bank members. The regional members took up the remaining 60 percent of authorized capital in the following amounts (U.S. dollars): Jamaica, $11.2 mil-lion; Trinidad and Tobago, $7.7 million; Bahamas, $3.3 million; Guyana, $2.4 million; Barbados, $1.4 million; British Honduras, $500,000; Grenada, $500,000; St. Lucia, $500,000; Antigua, $500,000; St. Vincent, $500,000; Dominica, $500,000; St. Kitts-Nevis-Anguilla, $500,000; Montserrat, British Virgin Islands, Cayman Islands, Turks and Caicos Islands, $500,000.[39]

Relative to Commonwealth Caribbean population of about four million, the resources of the Bank are substantial. As an enterprise, the Bank is quite capable of developing its own thrust; in fact, under the leadership of its first president, Sir Arthur Lewis, there can be little doubt that this is precisely what the Bank is doing. Sir Arthur has fairly strong and reasoned views about the Bank's role. They fit rather closely with those of Demas, who has an informal relationship with the Bank.

The Caribbean Development Bank is apt to shape its own direction and build upon its rather strong financial base. That direction may not always comport with what some of the Bank members may think best in the pursuit of their own national goals. Yet what Canada has done is not subject to retraction. Canada has played a large part in building a financial institution which, in time, can have an important role to play in the kind of economic and social structure that will evolve in the Caribbean. The implication in the Canadian Senate Committee report that the slate once marked could, if events demanded, be wiped clean, lacks validity. There are some kinds of aid programs that can be stopped without their function coming to an end.

A brief survey of loans made by the Bank through October 1971, and Canada's aid program in relation to the Bank, are revealing. Two loans totaling E.C. $2 million ($1 million U.S.) were made to the small island of St. Lucia. By far the largest loan, totaling $1.5 million was to fund the construction of a 102-room hotel; another $500,000 went to St. Lucia's Agricultural and Industrial Bank for supervised farm improvement loans to small farmers. Again, to St. Vincent, to a single borrower, the Bank extended E.C. $272,000 to build a 20-room hotel and only $166,000 to the island's Development Corporation "to build factory space for rental to small industries." Except for the British Honduran (Belize) Electricity Board, which received $3.05 million for electricity generation and distribution, the single 102-room hotel in St. Lucia had the largest loan. By October 1971, the Bank had made 14 loans totaling about E.C. $9 million.

If the $9 million total were studied in terms of agriculture, half (seven) of the total number of loans made were granted largely to nation-state agricultural development banks. The dollar total is also impressive relative to loans granted. It amounts to nearly E.C. $2.9 million. And the moneys went largely to the smaller islands.

Does this mean that the Bank is after all concerned with agricultural development on these islands? Is the single resort loan to be seen only as an unusual occurrence, not really reflecting Bank direction? The answer may come from an analysis of Canadian International Development Agency (CIDA) reports. In a document titled "Canada and The Developing World, 1970-71," CIDA spoke of the Commonwealth Caribbean. A prefatory section contains the general comment: "The [local] governments have found difficulties in agreeing on priorities in regional matters." Then, several pages later, CIDA takes note of the Agricultural Development Fund:

A $5 million agricultural development fund for the Commonwealth Caribbean was established in 1970-71,

and an agreement has been signed with the Caribbean
Development Bank to administer half the fund, which
will be provided to the Bank in the form of an advance.
The Bank will use this money for agricultural credit
projects in the less developed member countries,
including the Leeward and Windward Islands and Belize.
The remaining $2.5 million is expected to be used for
special agricultural projects in any of the countries in
the Caribbean currently receiving bilateral assistance
from CIDA.[40]

Can it be that the loans made by the Bank were in reality advances
from a special fund established by Canada? If so, why did the fund
have to be established? Would the Bank have been unwilling or unable
to make the noted loans otherwise? What rationale impels the administration of the fund by the Bank, particularly where regional priorities
cannot easily be arrived at by consensus? To what extent is Canada
forcing regionalism in the face of national aspirations?

It is not without meaning that economic regionalism, accepted
in principle, has been rejected in implementation for ten years. It is
one matter for tiny Grenada to accede to regionalism in principle, and
then ask: "Does regionalism mean that Jamaicans will take jobs from
us or make us their menials?" In this context there is something to
be learned from the $5 million agricultural development fund. Consider
the background to its establishment.

On April 17, 1970, the Canadian government revoked its de facto
$1.2 million annual rebate to Commonwealth Caribbean sugar produc-
ers. The rebate was replaced by the $5 million agricultural develop-
ment fund.

Although the new sum was larger, it was tied to particular projects that required negotiation. The Caribbean
governments gave considerable public evidence of annoy-
ance, a sentiment loudly echoed in the streets. Their
Premiers passed a resolution deprecatory of the Canadian action. Ostensibly they objected to the lack of
consultation, but actually it was the inability to use the
money as they saw fit that bothered them. They would
prefer their own development funds, not joint control
funds.[41]

The sugar rebate was a subsidy that flowed directly to nation-
states. It was a sum that could be used as a nation-state saw fit. The
development grant must be used for agricultural development, it cannot simply be used to fund a government for debt for a sugar crop
that did poorly.

By participating in the Caribbean Development Bank, by substituting development funds for direct subsidies, Canada is articulating a value system. That value system has as its primary goals (1) regionalism, and (2) the development of economically viable endeavors. To a Canadian, to those of developed countries, these goals are hardly subject to attack. But each of the goals demands short-term and long-term costs that those who are to be part of the regional system must pay. Initially, there is the wrenching effect of using land and people efficiently for agricultural production. On the part of the larger islands this may mean opening their markets to the produce of smaller islands, of allowing the smaller islands, for certain purposes, to be the suppliers of agricultural goods. For the smaller islands this may require redirection from single-crop production such as sugar or bananas to intense, diversified crop production. For both the large and small islands there would be some initial displacement, some insecurity as new techniques were learned and new markets opened.

CARIFTA: REGIONALISM AND THE BENEFITS OF FREE TRADE

The larger islands with their deeper economy can more easily absorb change; they can accept more readily disturbances in one sector that can be blunted by successes in another sector. For the smaller islands, regionalism is not always equivalent to their economic growth. They can, by way of illustration, point to the general trade statistics of the Caribbean Free Trade Association (Carifta), established in 1968 and bringing together in a free trade area twelve former territories of Great Britain.[42] The agreement, signed in Antigua, included as signatories by 1971 the following governments: Antigua, Barbados, Guyana, Dominica, Grenada, St. Kitts-Nevis-Anguilla, St. Lucia, St. Vincent, Jamaica, Montserrat, British Honduras, Trinidad and Tobago.

The objectives of the Association, set out in the agreement, include: the promotion of expansion and diversification of trade in the area; insuring that trade between member states takes place on the basis of fair competition; encouragement of balanced and progressive development of area economies; fostering harmonious and liberalized trade between member states; and insuring an equitable distribution of the benefits flowing from such policies. To achieve these ends the Association has sought to eliminate tariff barriers and quantitative restrictions on intraregional trade. In addition, through special protocols on oil and fats and agricultural marketing, the Association has allocated markets for the surpluses of designated commodities produced especially in the less developed areas.

The Association, in which each member state holds one vote only, was designed to be a first step toward economic integration. It was hoped that the principles laid down in "Annex A" of the Carifta agreement would come to fruition. These include: the adoption of a common external tariff; the establishment of regional industries; a strategy for the location of industries recognizing the special needs of the less developed member states; the harmonization of fiscal incentives for the establishment of these industries; and the improvement of intraregional shipping services.

The scheme was grand. It was shaped to allow all member states to grow more closely together, and was to a considerable extent a scheme of self-help. Now that it is a few years old, the time may be appropriate to inquire into the vitality of Carifta. Has there developed greater trade volume within the Association? Have regional disparities been softened? Have the smaller member states benefited? Is there now consensus for economic integration?

The facts are not comforting. Carifta has grown, but it remains minuscule next to Canada, the United Kingdom, or the United States. To demonstrate the point, let us consider two island states, Barbados and Trinidad and Tobago. In 1969 Barbados imported from Canada goods valued at E.C. $21,526,935 ($10,763,467 U.S.) and exported goods to Canada in the amount of $2,685,548 ($1,342,774 U.S.) The Barbadian imports of Canadian goods, though somewhat less in value than 1968, still was considerably higher than the 1965 total of $14,165,497.

Canadian sales to Barbados were about the same as the total of all imports from Caribbean countries to Barbados, namely, $21,579,543 for 1969. This was significantly more than in 1968 when the value of all Caribbean imports to Barbados was $17,130,859.

Now add United Kingdom imports to Barbados. In 1969 they totaled $56,158,529, a figure far higher than the year before when they reached $45,888,990. Barbadian export to the U.K. for 1969 was $27,797,770, down nearly $9 million from the year before. But even Barbadian exports to the U.K. were far greater than the sum total of its exports to all Caribbean countries, which in 1969 was $14,639,431, nearly a 20 percent increase over 1968. For the United States the story is about the same. U. S. sales in 1969 to Barbados were $43,636,719 while imports were only $16,616,814.

Even in terms of Carifta growth it is not the small islands that have benefited. On the contrary, in almost every instance the smaller islands have lost significant ground. Contrasted with 1967 or 1968, 1969 found Barbados importing far less from Grenada, St. Lucia, St. Vincent, or St. Kitts. But with the help of Carifta, Barbados has measurably increased its exports to these islands. The statistics are shown in Table 9.

TABLE 9

Barbadian Imports from and Exports to Dominica,
Grenada, St. Kitts, and St. Lucia, 1967-69
(in E.C. dollars)

	Dominica	Grenada	St. Kitts	St. Lucia
Imports				
1967	256,916	18,528	27,996	915,310
1968	339,621	5,721	37,475	906,710
1969	211,294	17,519	9,003	551,648
Exports				
1967	838,456	1,192,103	741,369	1,785,589
1968	972,870	1,558,125	897,434	1,867,440
1969	1,210,458	1,671,068	952,839	2,165,497

Source: West Indies and Caribbean Year Book 1972, p. 114.

Barbadian exports were spread among many islands. Its imports, however, in dollar value, were centered on only three: Guyana, Jamaica, and Trinidad. Of these Trinidad accounted for the largest amount, $13,296,403, for more than half of all Caribbean imports.

The picture for Trinidad and Tobago is much the same as that of Barbados. The Economist Intelligence Unit reported in 1972 of the Trinidad and Tobago's 1971 trading experience (see Table 10):

> An interesting feature, in the first half of last year, was the much lower rate of growth of imports from the Carifta region—1.5 percent compared with Trinidad and Tobago's overall 17.9 percent. This is not unexpected, in view of the country's dependence on non-Carifta sources for the crude oil and capital equipment which make up some two-thirds of its overseas purchases, and the rapid price rise in the first of these sectors.
>
> On the export side, however, the Carifta market grew by a firm 10.8 percent, as Trinidad and Tobago's light industry is sufficiently developed for trade to reflect the progressive reduction of tariffs on manu-factures within Carifta. A significant feature . . . is that the most sophisticated market in the region, Jamaica, showed the most dynamic growth. Indeed, exports to the area classified as less-developed—i.e.,

TABLE 10

Trinidad and Tobago Trade with the Caribbean Free Trade Area

	January-June 1970		1971	
	T.T.$ (millions)	%	T.T.$ (millions)	%
Exports (total)	45.6	100.0	53.8	100.0
Guyana	15.5	34.0	17.9	33.3
Jamaica	5.7	12.5	9.2	17.1
Barbados	8.3	18.2	8.9	16.5
Imports (total)	13.5	100.0	13.7	100.0
Guyana	6.5	48.1	6.5	47.5
Jamaica	4.0	29.6	4.7	34.3
Barbados	1.0	7.4	1.6	11.7

Source: QER: The West Indies, Bahamas, Bermuda, British Honduras, Guyana, No. 1-1972 (London: The Economist Intelligence Unit, 1972), p. 11.

the Associated States and dependencies—rose by only 1.2 percent.[43]

Regionalism is not bringing either economic or political integration to the Commonwealth Caribbean. The larger islands of Jamaica, Barbados, and Trinidad have benefited from Carifta. The smaller member states of, for example, Grenada and St. Lucia have not shared substantially in that benefit. In 1970 and 1971 a move was made to seek again the political union that had failed ten years before as the United Kingdom released its hold on the Commonwealth Caribbean. On November 1, 1971, six nation-states signed the Declaration of Grenada, a document intended to achieve political integration. The Economist Intelligence Unit said of the declaration one year later:

> Support for the Declaration of Grenada, which provides for a political union of the British Caribbean islands, had already begun to slip away within days of its formal publication, on November 1. Two of the original six signatories (Guyana, and the Associated States other than Antigua) have withdrawn from the programme outlined in the declaration. Both Grenada and St. Vincent consider that Trinidad and Tobago's decision not to join and Barbados's absence throughout make

the scheme meaningless. The four remaining countries are proceeding with a slightly revised timetable: a preparatory commission is to be established by February 1, 1972 (not end-December 1971, as originally planned) and a constitutional assembly subsequently established (not by June 1, 1972, as first intended) to draft a constitution, which is not now likely to have been promulgated by the earlier target date of April 22, 1973.

The state's prospects seem worse than ever. While the predominant Guyana is ready to lead, it is very unlikely that the Associated States will be ready to follow. Moreover, even if the opposition were to win the election in Jamaica this year and bring the island into discussions on Caribbean Federation, the accession of Carifta's "giant" would only reinforce the smaller islands' fears that their political and economic objectives would go by the board in a regional state.[44]

What seems to be emerging is increased trade between the larger states of the Commonwealth Caribbean, though by no means nearly enough to offset major dependence on Canada, the United Kingdom, and the United States, their traditional trading partners. Yet even increased trade between the larger island states, stimulated in part by Carifta, has not brought economic integration or political union. For example, each of the large nation-states maintains its own currency and central bank operation. This is true of Jamaica, Trinidad and Tobago, the Bahamas, and more recently Barbados.

The smaller island nations, concerned with their economic future, have been excluded from even the subregional economic groupings. Barbados, which once stood as the anchor for the Eastern Caribbean Currency Authority, has left the currency exchange and its member Associated States which consist of the small islands such as Grenada and St. Lucia. Barbados is going its own way with its own central bank.

Pointing to the isolation of the smaller island states and their poverty relative to the rest of the Commonwealth Caribbean, some have argued for increased Canadian aid to the Leeward and Windward Islands. Regionalism, the argument runs, can hardly go forward when the per capita income of the smaller islands is only one-third the average income of Trinidad and one-half that of Jamaica. Moreover, it is not a good sign for regionalism when there are unemployed in Barbados or Antigua who will not cut sugar cane because the work is thought demeaning and St. Lucian labor is imported to do the job.[45]

If regionalism is to be achieved the gap between rich and poor must be narrowed. The questions are how this is to be achieved and at what price. It would take relatively little of Canada's foreign aid to bring major impact on the smaller islands. But what direction should that aid take? The social costs connected with extensive tourist development might outweigh the economic benefits. Agricultural development must have direction. Should the traditional crops of sugar and bananas be intensified? Or should diversification be sought? Again, the answers depend not only upon available markets but a willingness on the part of local government and its citizens to accept the social costs of change.

This much is certain: Building an infrastructure in advance of a decision on the kind of economy an island might select may impel hasty actions later regretted. For St. Lucia, with Canadian aid, to enlarge its airport facilities, build new roads, and establish a general educational structure is to saddle itself with direct costs that later might prove unacceptable. Airports and highways must be maintained by personnel, equipment, and materials. For a nation with limited resources the airport must find a way of producing revenue; the highways must serve an economic purpose. On the day the airport and roads open, pressures mount for the production of income. Both tourism and industry must be encouraged, and long-range planning must assume a position of diminishing priority. And yet for a small nation with a very limited land mass and a large population, there is little room for error in estimating and accepting social costs.

ESTABLISHING AN EDUCATIONAL INFRASTRUC-
TURE THROUGH AID FUNDS

The need to plan before acting assumes major importance in education. It is fair to ask whether the nations of the Commonwealth Caribbean or the aid-granting nations such as Canada have asked questions relating to the kind of educational system that would best fulfill the aspirations of the island states. Indeed, one suspects that both the island states and Canada assumed the need for primary and secondary educational system that would necessarily be good and efficient if modeled along Canadian or British lines.

Canadian aid to primary and secondary education throughout the Commonwealth Caribbean has been extensive on a government-to-government and a regional basis. Effort has gone into human and material assistance. Consider, by way of example, the year 1969-70. Jamaica was given 91 teachers, advisers, and trainees at a cost of $1,025,000. On the whole the aid money went to technical or vocational education. CIDA summarized the Jamaica expenditure in these terms:

A gradual shift in the education programme from primary teacher trainers in six Jamaican Teacher Training Colleges towards technical vocational education was introduced in September, 1969. Two technical teachers were assigned to the College of Arts, Science and Technology, three vocational teachers were assigned to the Technical High Schools and two advisers, one in technical education and one in vocational education, are assisting in establishing of a technical and vocational education administrative unit in the Ministry of Education. Two Canadian Home Economists to establish a Department of Home Economics in the Jamaica School of Agriculture have also been approved.

One adviser will continue to participate in an Organization and Methods training course for the Jamaican Civil Service in the current year. A civil aviation adviser is assisting in the operation of the Civil Aviation Department, while a second adviser is continuing to assist Jamaica in air negotiations as required. Arrangements have also been made for a Canadian microbiologist to advise in the establishment of a pure foods laboratory. A management expert has been assigned to the Jamaica Development Bank. An architect and interior designer are working in the Ministry of Education to establish designs for school and furniture construction which will be capable of production in Jamaica. Four instructors are serving at the Jamaica Hotel Training School. A Canadian forestry adviser has assisted in preparation of a forestation programme for the country.[46]

What was done in Jamaica was also done on a somewhat lesser scale in Trinidad and Tobago[47] (83 teachers, advisers and trainees at a cost of $855,000) and Barbados (44 at a cost of $320,000).[48] With some exceptions the aid personnel were to meet certain specific economic needs of the recipient nation-state. Thus, Canadian advisers, helpful in setting up a hotel school in Jamaica, did the same in Barbados where, in addition, an animal nutritionist was obtained to aid in the development of a dairy industry.

For the smaller islands with their less numerous populations, the Canadian educational aid thrust is relatively much stronger. For the Associated States of Antigua, St. Kitts, Dominica, St. Lucia, Grenada, St. Vincent, and Montserrat, $1,675,000 was allocated for 183 teachers, advisers and trainees. But, unlike Jamaica, Trinidad, and Barbados there was not the same specific, specialized tasks noted in the CIDA report.[49] In addition, heavy Canadian capital grants were made for the construction of primary and junior secondary schools (ages 5-15). Dominica received $850,000, and Antigua $790,000. As part of the capital grant program Canada allocated $2,800,000 for twenty prefabricated primary schools, each to be a one-story building containing ten classrooms, a library, and administrative facilities, and intended to accommodate 500 children between 6 and 12 years old.[50]

Educating a Technocracy

Canadian support for higher or secondary education has not been found wanting. The major recipient of such grants has been the University of the West Indies, the only "regional" institution established and continuing after the United Kingdom released its hold on the Commonwealth Caribbean. Indeed, the University of the West Indies can trace its beginnings to its status as the University College of the West Indies and the Royal Charter issued on January 9, 1949. University rank was obtained when a Royal Charter under the Great Seal of the Realm was granted on April 2, 1962.

The university, whose chancellor remains HRH Princess Alice, was designed as a regional institution to be physically present in the jurisdictions of all member states. The member states, in turn, constitute the university's governing council. The members include representatives of Grenada, Dominica, British Honduras, Montserrat, Jamaica, Antigua, Barbados, St. Lucia, Trinidad and Tobago, British Virgin Islands, St. Vincent, and St. Kitts.

Major campuses are located in the larger territories. Thus, the medical school with its teaching hospital is in Jamaica; the faculties of agriculture, engineering, and arts and sciences are in Trinidad and Tobago; the faculty of law is in Barbados. A Department of Extra-Mural Studies provides "adult education" on the smaller islands. As part of the department, extension centers have been developed on the smaller islands.

Canadian aid to the University of the West Indies has been extensive. Outright grants of $1 million each year were set aside for five years from 1967.

Through this program, Canada has continued to provide Canadian professors for the University staff, training in Canada for designated UWI staff members at the postgraduate level, and undergraduate training at the UWI for nominees from the Commonwealth Caribbean islands. . . . Further capital assistance is also being provided. Construction is being initiated of six university centres on six Eastern Caribbean islands, a 200-student residence in Barbados, and a faculty club in Trinidad.[51]

The number of Canadian professors sent to the Caribbean has been impressive; about twenty have gone each year. Moreover, Canada for the first time has provided scholarships in the Commonwealth Caribbean for West Indian students. This is the reverse of earlier policy which brought West Indians to Canada for education. The result of the new program, as stated by the Canadian Senate Committee, has been to slow the "brain drain" from the Caribbean to Canada and at the same time to be supportive of the University of the West Indies.[52]

Canada has helped to establish an educational infrastructure in the Commonwealth Caribbean. Of this there can be no doubt. The question is not whether the people or the recipient nations are grateful for what Canada has done. The issue is not, as one Canadian banker put it, "Let the people know that Canada is helping." It is not often that the recipient of a direct gift will be grateful to the giver—the mere fact that a gift had to be given is a comment on the stature and the capacity of the recipient, and it can tend to belittle.

What is significant is the relevance to national needs of what Canada is sponsoring and the extent to which Canada should impose its judgment on that of the recipient nation-state. Again, the picture that emerges is that of the larger states better able to particularize their needs and the mechanisms necessary to meet those needs. For the purpose of illustration, consider Trinidad and Tobago. In its third Five-Year Plan (1969-73) a draft education program for 1969 to 1983 was set forth.[53] An effort was made to state the purposes or goals of education. Education, said the report, has both an intrinsic and an instrumental value. The government recognized the need for helping in the development of the human personality. On the other hand, continued the report, the government is faced daily with serious economic and social problems of unemployment and underdevelopment. These problems must be resolved. The educational system must be shaped to assist in their resolution. Out of that system must come not only skilled personnel but also people trained to be "good" citizens.[54]

Yet, "good" citizens in a Trinidadian sense does not necessarily mean "good" citizens in a Canadian sense. Demas wrote:

In considering the development of the Caribbean economies we have to bear in mind two fundamental institutional constraints: the existence of political democracy
on classic Westminster lines and the existence of a strong
independent and forceful trade-union movement sharing
the philosophy of North American, and to a lesser degree,
British trade unionism. These constraints are not of
course unique to the Caribbean—although I suspect that
in few other underdeveloped countries is the trade-union
movement so imbued with ideas and attitudes more

119

appropriate to the advanced countries. This stems not
only from the commendable, though often misplaced,
idealism of certain international organizations but from
the close proximity to North America and the general
"openness" of the society which makes for very close
contacts with the trade union movements of Britain and
North America.[55]

The tensions and restraints that can operate on a developing
country because of political democracy and the possibility of alternative government are not insubstantial. There will be brought to the
fore the quite justifiable demands of the populace for immediate and
badly needed improvements, especially in social services. Since
resources are always limited, this can conflict with long-run government objectives for growth and structural changes in the economy.
In addition, trade unions often do pursue policies for short-term gains
in real wages and working conditions for their membership at the
expense of the expansion of employment opportunities, capital formation, and government budget.[56]

Demas argues as an economist. He makes the point that the
parliamentary democracy and trade unionism of the advanced countries are the products rather than the concomitants of the developed
process. They are what a country can afford after it is developed.
This is not to say that parliamentary democracy and trade unionism
lack redeeming virtue. According to Demas the trade union does
effectively represent a portion of the population, and by so doing it
can play a positive role by giving dignity to the wage relationship,
promoting productivity, inculcating discipline, providing welfare
facilities, and mobilizing savings from its members for national economic growth.[57]

What Trinidad and Tobago, one of the most developed of the
Commonwealth Caribbean countries, is striking for is a balance in
its educational system. It wants citizens who will respond to national
need, who will discipline themselves so that the nation might grow.
It does not want the value system of North American, of Canadian
parliamentary democracy, of Canadian trade unionism, transplanted
in Trinidad.

For Canada, a major provider of human resources, there is a
fundamental question: Can Canada provide the people who are sophisticated enough to strike the balance, the "restrained" democracy,
sought by Trinidad? To send Canadians to Trinidad or bring Trinidadians to Canada and hold out the Canadian value system is to ignore
recipient nation needs. The end result is that of Canada imposing a
system on Trinidad.

120

What applies to Trinidad is valid for the smaller states. For the mini-nations of Grenada, St. Lucia, or Antigua, their position may be even more difficult than Trinidad. They may not be able to define their needs with the same precision. In such a situation, Canada as a dispenser of aid must do more than supply teachers; it must help the recipient articulate its own educational goals.

Trinidad and Tobago is moving toward a resolution of its educational problems. Emphasis is being placed on vocational and technical training. The third five-year plan states:

> One of the fundamental requirements for the economic future of Trinidad and Tobago is a skilled and employable labour force adequate in numbers and in competence. The educational system of Trinidad and Tobago has traditionally been dominated by primary schooling for the vast majority and classically oriented secondary education for the very few. In the hope of widening intellectual horizons and as a matter of national economic survival, the Plan for Technical Education aims to bring Trinidad and Tobago into the stream of present developments in Science and Technology in order that industry will be supplied with persons possessing developed intellectual resources, certain fundamental skills and a flexibility for further education. The present pace of scientific and industrial change is such as to place a premium not on specialized training in specific skills but upon basic education and general technical education with the aim of promoting adaptability based upon a thorough understanding of the processes involved.[58]

Focusing upon the university, the government set forth priorities: (1) Trinidad and Tobago should develop sufficiently adequate facilities to meet national needs in the fields of engineering, agriculture, and arts and sciences. (2) With regard to arts and sciences, the government will place emphasis on considerably increasing the number of students entering a science program as contrasted with an arts program. Again, more teachers and enlarged physical plant are needed. (3) During the Third Five-Year Plan, courses in geography and education will be introduced. An attempt will be made to strengthen a capacity for accountancy. Research centers will be established for industrial affairs, food and nutrition, and the use of local materials for construction activities.[59]

The priorities of Trinidad and Tobago really go to only one matter, building an efficient technocracy. Competent people must be trained, able to assist government in making and implementing decisions. That is the first need, the first goal of the educational system. That is precisely what Trinidad and Tobago lack even by the government's own admission:

> The failure of the country to develop at a rapid enough rate the managerial expertise necessary to operate the economy has reflected itself in an oppressive bureaucracy with overburdening of a few, a quantitative and not a qualitative growth in the public sector, and a resort to criteria other than merit for employment in the private sector.[60]

The government has moved to create the mechanisms that will provide the needed managerial expertise. At the University of the West Indies it established a Department of Business Management in the Second Five-Year Development Plan (1964-68). In addition, it established a Labor College and a Management Training and Productivity Center. Within the Civil Service itself a Central Training Unit was established, and staff were given leaves for study. All of this was done through foreign aid.[61]

In the Third Five-Year Plan, (1969-73), published in 1970, more foreign aid was to be sought in order to establish an Institute of Management and Administration Studies. The Institute

> . . . will provide practical training, consulting services, seminars and workshops in the field of Business Management so as to provide a steady stream of top and middle level management for the private sector and public corporations. It will also provide an opportunity for the Civil Servant to be exposed to the modern techniques of business management not only with a view to upgrading his ability in his own field but also to facilitate the constant interaction between Civil Servant and businessman and vice versa.[62]

The need for a competent technocracy in Trinidad and throughout the Commonwealth Caribbean is great. Trinidad, like the other Commonwealth Caribbean nations, has opted not so much for regionalism as nationalism, which in turn has been interpreted in the harsh terms of "Trinidad for Trinidadians." Foreign ownership of local enterprise is being discouraged, and local participation encouraged. Even more important, expatriate employees from managers to menials are being denied work permits. Their jobs are to go to nationals. But, particularly for the technocracy, it is vital that the nationals be trained.

The end result for Trinidad as for the rest of the Commonwealth Caribbean is the sudden opening of numerous responsible positions in the private sector. Because of government intervention in the economy, the same kinds of openings are available in the public sector. Once the supply of talent is limited to nationals, the question must be asked: What mechanism can be devised to yield qualified personnel?

Taking as an example the banks of Trinidad, foreign or national, without exception they will not look to the University of the West Indies as a desirable source for personnel. Their need is immediate, not distant. People must be found now, not later. They cannot close their business while people are trained. In a sense, the Canadian banks are under even more pressure—from local government, and, for example, from the Senate of Canada, which through a committee advised:

> All companies operating in the Caribbean should recog-
> nize the need to recruit locally for staff positions at all
> levels. Canadian companies should not only adhere to
> the requirements of local governments, but can greatly
> increase the effectiveness of their operations by ener-
> getically recruiting local personnel, particularly for
> managerial and supervisory positions. The practice of
> recruiting Commonwealth Caribbean students and other
> expatriates in Canada is an excellent one which should
> be expanded.[63]

It is one matter to speak of the general use of students. It is quite another matter to designate a recent commerce graduate as a trust officer handling the personal affairs and perhaps millions of dollars of a non-national's money. Aside from the trust officer, there is the manager of the bank itself; the qualities of discretion and responsibility to client come not after months, but after years of experience. To foist upon the financial institutions and the banks, which dominate the heights of an economy, inexperienced leadership may compel a nation to pay a very high price in loss of confidence for very short-term rewards.

In saying this a further observation must be made: Why weren't nationals trained to positions of leadership years ago? The Canadian banks, the largest of Canada's global corporations, have been doing business in the Caribbean for more than 50 years. The answer is fairly clear. It was thought proper to have Canadian banks staffed, at all levels, by Canadian or English personnel. Only with the coming of independence in the 1960s and direct pressure from the newly established governments have Canadian bank employment practices changed.

The difficulty now is that the kind of change demanded by the new governments exceeds the capacity of the educational system. And to place unqualified persons in positions of major responsibility is to invite harm to the nation itself.

Trinidad and Tobago is seeking an answer to its manpower problem by creating an educational infrastructure along Western lines. That is, the university and its formal curriculum, directed to more specific areas such as business administration, have been designated as the mechanism for producing a technocracy. Barbados and Jamaica are also using this approach. And Canada is a major supporter of the university. Why? Is the university socially or economically valuable to the Caribbean? Will it provide the technocracy needed? And does Canada have an obligation to point out some of the social and economic costs of the university?

Resolution of these questions may come from a restatement of the purposes of education: Education is a means for inculcating those rules, beliefs, and standards necessary for a society to exist. Related to this, education conveys the knowledge necessary to perform certain jobs. This knowledge extends from such widely needed skills as reading, writing, and arithmetic to training in farming, engineering, and even banking. Having said this, must it be assumed that the only information system capable of delivering that needed at the highest level is the university?

> In addition to the content of education, there is the question of the means by which education is accomplished. A costly education diverts economic resources and educated manpower from other uses and thus impedes an increase in living standards. If education is financed through taxes, an expensive educational program may significantly hamper a self-feeding process of improvement in economic efficiency by diverting resources from the financing of economic innovation.
>
> Formalization of education, although it may in some cases be essential for efficiency, raises problems for societal control over the content of the education. Where the content of education is governed by a class of educators, by the members of a profession, by self-perpetuating faculties of universities, or by religious or ethnic groups, the content of the education may not correspond to societal needs. Education may sometimes be the means for reforming a society, but it also can contribute to perpetuating the society's problems and deficiencies.64

In opting for the university, for the "school" system, did Trinidad and Tobago, the other Commonwealth Caribbean countries, or Canada consider alternatives? If so, how was the choice to be made? Is there a rationale for quantifying and objectifying the costs and benefits of an educational delivery system? In the 1960s, at the time the Commonwealth Caribbean was first obtaining its independence from the United Kingdom, economists articulated "the investment-in-human-capital appraoch."[65] Education is a form of investment in human capital. The rate of return to society can be estimated from the cross-sectional relations between differentials in education and income. Among the points at issue in this approach is why there is a relationship—should one be found—between education and income. To what extent, for example, is power derived from an in-group status, a situation historically not uncommon to the United Kingdom? John Culbertson comments:

> The problem becomes yet more intractable when the preferred position of the educated comes about not through any formally defined educational requirements but through informal preference shown by educated people to other educated people, even with reference to positions that do not require the education. This situation leads to what might be termed an "education prejudice," the effects of which are similar to those of racial prejudice in limiting the opportunities of the inferior group relative to those of the superior group, of altering the rules of the game, the terms of trade, between them. Quantitative analysis of this matter seems well beyond the capabilities of existing methodology. Yet the effects of such side effects of education may be important.
>
> In low-income countries, where the role of higher education as a qualification for admittance to an elite status is established even more firmly than in most Western nations, the error in inferring the social productivity of additional education from the income advantage of the educated is especially great. The existence of the "educated unemployed," a situation that has existed in India since the era of British rule, evidently implies that the marginal social productivity of enlarging the numbers educated in the existing way within the existing societal rules may be zero (negative after allowance for educational costs), even though the educated employed enjoy large incomes.[66]

It may well be that the approach suggested by Culbertson is the more meaningful course: Eliminate the use of formal education as a basis for market power. The university or high school degree would no longer become important; it would no longer become either the test or the mandate for employment. Rather, employment would be offered on the basis of ability to perform the job.

Applied to the Commonwealth Caribbean in very specific terms, perhaps the educational emphasis might well be within the private sector itself. The scenario is not difficult, and, above all, it is not expensive either in social or economic costs. Again, consider on-the-job training as applied to Canadian banks. Within the period of only a few years—once the policy was accepted by top management—a total shift in personnel from the teller to the intermediate management level (the sub-branch manager) took place. Working patiently, throughout the Caribbean literally hundreds of new employees entered the labor force assuming positions never before handled by nationals. Not infrequently those seeking employment or promotion were not qualified by Canadian standards. While accepted Canadian or North American tests for proficiency were given, the results were read liberally.

The Canadian banks and the banking industry generally were able to attract the best talent in the Caribbean, for a banking job carries with it prestige as well as a good income. Literally hundreds of applicants might seek a single banking job on any given island. The result has been that relatively highly motivated and reasonably well-educated persons have moved as nationals into banking positions. Training for specific functions, whether teller or sub-branch manager, has taken place on the job through a flexible combination of experience and tutoring.

Is it not possible to use the same flexible on-the-job approach to middle and even top management? Why couldn't competent, motivated sub-branch managers be trained to full positions of middle and top management? Donald Fleming, Managing Director of the Bank of Nova Scotia Trust Company in the Bahamas, spoke in 1972 to the questions raised: He noted that the banks and trust companies in the Bahamas employ about 2,300 persons, 80 percent of whom are Bahamians. Their salary scales were the highest in the Bahamas, and materially higher than those prevailing in Canada, the United Kingdom, or the United States:

> The quality of the employment record of the financial
> community is as important as its quantitative features in
> the Bahamian economy at this state of its development.
> It is the financial institutions which are largely respon-
> sible for imparting sophistication to the economy of this
> country, for they are the principal channel of contact
> with business abroad. They offer opportunity to young
> Bahamians to take preferred employment. They provide
> training in almost every conceivable way, through courses,
> on-the-job training, and day-by-day instruction. They
> offer inducements to their staffs to study for the diploma
> of the Institute of Bankers and other institutes of high

standing, contributing to the cost of tuition and textbooks, and donating substantial cash awards to those who successfully pass the examinations. They plan to sponsor a banking and financial library to facilitate study by their staffs.

The value of the training imparted to their employees is perhaps best attested to by the fact that their staffs have been constantly raided by other employers, including Government departments, seeking competent trained staff. The best standards of training and business practice to be found in the Bahamas today owe much to the banks and trust companies.

The sophisticated type of modern operation carried on by many of the large financial institutions operating in Nassau requires a considerable proportion of highly trained personnel. Indeed, the function performed by the major trust companies, for example, is in many respects of a professional nature. The type of qualification and training required for personnel is therefore very advanced.[67]

Fleming said many things: (1) He attested to the banks' capacity to educate using either the resources of a bank, or its trade association affiliate (the Institute of Bankers), or collective action by several banks (the establishment of a financial library). (2) In some areas the banks have been successful. A manifestation of that success has been the desire of government to "raid" the banks for employees.

The situation described in the Bahamas applies as well in Jamaica, Barbados, Trinidad and Tobago, and the Associated States. Government has gone to the banks for civil servants. It is not unusual to find former private bank employees in the central bank or economic planning units of any of the island states. In Trinidad, for example, the Workers' Bank, established as a partnership largely between the trade unions and the government, has senior staff who had been private bank employees. Moreover, the government, having in fact expropriated the Bank of Montreal and established a new national bank, gave operative control to a highly skilled person who received considerable experience (that is, education) as the secretary for the nation's central bank.

What concerned Fleming was not the educational program but rather the time lag between education and qualification. If the government insisted on a program requiring the exclusive employment of nationals, and if the nationals were not yet ready to assume positions of major responsibility, then business was bound to be lost in the Bahamas. Fleming wanted a more flexible work permit policy allowing for freer use of expatriates for longer periods of time. He did not mention in his public presentation that not one Bahamian had yet completed the Institute of Bankers course for senior trust officers. This he disclosed in a private interview.

A New Program of Education: A Positive Role for Canada's Banks

For Canada, a more meaningful type of aid program might well be directed to its own financial institutions in the Commonwealth Caribbean. Why couldn't assistance and encouragement be forthcoming for the educational effort in which the banks and their trust companies are engaged? Both in terms of quality and quantity the results could be most beneficial to the host countries, which recognize the importance of the financial institutions. Millions of dollars need not be placed in concrete structures, in capital plant and equipment removed physically and realistically from the economic life of the land. For potential payout to the Commonwealth Caribbean, would there not be a great deal gained by training and qualifying those in middle-management positions for top management of Canadian banks?

The framework presently exists to make such an educational effort meaningful: (1) Canadian banks in a very short period of time have trained hundreds of Caribbean nationals for clerical and middle management positions. (2) On the whole, the training procedures were created and executed by the banks themselves, at times using correspondence courses. The educational system of the university was not involved. (3) The Canadian banks (and most other foreign banks) have committed themselves not only to equity participation by nationals in the Commonwealth Caribbean but to majority control by those nationals. (4) This implies that in time direction and management of Canadian banks in the Commonwealth Caribbean will be by nationals of the nation-states where they are incorporated. Accordingly, the Canadian Senate Committee on Foreign Affairs stated:

> The other main sector of Canadian corporate activity, financial institutions, is an intrinsically sensitive one. It will be increasingly important for these firms to continue policies of encouraging local equity participation and developing local personnel resources. They will also be required to meet growing demands that their operations be closely geared to the development needs of the Caribbean communities.[68]

In more general terms, the position taken by the Canadian Senate Committee on Foreign Relations is reflected in the position of the government of Canada. In late 1968, as part of its overall review of

128

foreign policy, the government initiated a comprehensive review of Canadian policies in international development assistance. That study was completed and published in 1970. Of the private sector's role, the study concluded that Canadian business and industry

> . . . may have a growing role of particular importance in the development programme. A number of recipient countries now wish to increase and diversify their sources of capital, and many are at a stage in their development which require small-scale and medium-scale industrial enterprises. Canadian experience with this scale of operation . . . is often particularly relevant to their requirements. The Government will therefore initiate further measures to encourage Canadian business and industry to establish or expand operations in the developing countries by helping to overcome the special factors that lie in their way, while at the same time bearing in mind the problems that can arise from an indiscriminate application of such resources.[69]

A number of programs were established to implement government policy. Within CIDA, the Business and Industry Division in 1970 began funding starter and feasibility studies of Canadian firms considering the establishment of business in developing countries. While the amount of starter assistance is limited to $2,500, more than 30 Canadian firms sought such aid during the first six months of the program's operation.[70] It is the Division's function, primarily through aid and information, to lessen fear of Canadian business in establishing abroad. It is the intent of CIDA to increase the investment flow of Canada's private sector to the developing world. To CIDA, the private sector is not doing enough. On a ten-year average, total investment of private industry throughout the world to developing nations averaged $3.69 billion (U.S. billions) annually in the 1960s. Of this figure, the Canadian part amounted to $52 million annually.[71]

To cushion the blow of possible expropriation, of war, revolution, insurrection, of prohibitions against the repatriation of investment, the Canadian government established the Export Development Corporation. As a crown corporation, investment insurance is provided against noncommercial or political risks. The work of the corporation is keyed directly to Canadian aid policy: investment insurance will only be provided if the business enterprise will complement Canada's development assistance objectives and will be of commercial and industrial advantage to Canada.[72]

The work of the Business and Industry Division of CIDA and that of the Export Development Corporation is to stimulate Canadian private investment in developing countries. Considered quite apart from the investment incentive program is the role of CIDA in education. CIDA has a special relationship with two agencies, Canadian University Service Overseas (CUSO) and Canadian Executive Service Overseas (CESO). Created in 1960, CUSO had by 1970 nearly 1,200 persons working abroad in more than 40 countries. Largely, CUSO provides teachers in primary, secondary, and post-secondary schools. Its greatest concentration is in mathematics and the sciences.[73] Of CESO, CIDA stated:

> CESO came into existence to enlist the experience and expertise of Canadian business and industry for international development. It makes available to the developing countries, in response to specific requests and on their terms, modern management techniques to help them to develop their resources and economic potential more fully and efficiently.
>
> Since 1968 it has completed nearly 300 assignments in 36 different countries, mostly on a short-term basis, and it plans to send nearly 200 volunteers abroad in the current year.
>
> Although CESO began operations by using primarily retired executives, it has turned increasingly to managers in the middle and senior levels of Canadian business and industry. It is gratifying that more and more Canadian firms are releasing executives for short-term assignments overseas. For they recognize a mutual benefit in the scheme: these assignments not only enable Canadian business and industry to contribute to international development; they also enhance a man's career, and this in turn benefits his own country.[74]

Both the investment incentive and the educational programs of Canadian foreign aid could be slightly modified to maximize the use of the private sector, and in the Commonwealth Caribbean, the use of the Canadian banks as an educational institution. Indeed, working with the Canadian government, with CIDA, a formal program could be developed by the banks individually or jointly. Surely, at least some of the mathematics teachers of CUSO could be funneled to the Canadian banks to be supportive of company training for clerical positions such as tellers. And CESO might prove the appropriate program to bring, at the request of host countries, highly sophisticated, recently retired Canadian bank and trust officers to train recruits to senior management in the Caribbean. What is more, as part of the training of senior management, CIDA rather than the banks themselves could urge the transfer of Caribbean nationals throughout the Caribbean so that they might obtain deeper experience and broader perspective.

The end result of a proper training program might be to allow the Canadian banks to "Caribbeanize" more quickly. While they might continue to have difficulty selling a majority of their equity, they might be able to transfer effective management. And out of the creativity of that management might come the kinds of proposals that would go far beyond the benefits of equity ownership. On each of the island states there might emerge the kind of competent technocracy that can address itself to the needs of a particular area and at the same time have the capacity to search out sources in and beyond the island state to resolve those needs.

There is precedent for these proposals. In the 1950s the American aid program allocated a small sum, barely $1 million, to form management associations and institutes throughout Latin America. It was indeed a very small sum relative to the hundreds of millions of dollars spent through the Alliance for Progress. The management association program was neither embraced by the United States nor the Latin America governments, which could point to organizations in abundance. Why fund another organization?

But the management association program did have an effect. It responded to a young generation's felt need to manage its own affairs. The association helped to create competence, demands, and self-respect. Peter F. Drucker reports on the effect of the program in Colombia:

> Out of this apparently insignificant support for management associations came, for instance, the upsurge of development in the Cauca Valley of Colombia, in and around the city of Cali. The young men who met in the courses of the new Colombian management association rapidly organized themselves to take responsibility for the local university, the Universidad del Valle. There they pushed a public health program which, for the first time in the whole region, is systematically training and organizing villagers for public health. They started a series of management courses—especially courses for the top management people in which the most successful citizens of the area went to school (something almost unimaginable to an older generation of Latin Americans), and in which each of their businesses was examined, diagnosed, and prescribed for by the whole group. Then they began to supply young and well-trained people to local governments, both in state and city.
>
> Cali is still poor; and unemployment is still too high. But out of the work at the Universidad del Valle have come

at least 30,000 jobs in the last ten years. More important, out of it has come an entirely different leadership—for the entire community and for all major community activities.[75]

The multinational corporation need not be an engine for evil. It can bring positive good. It can materially assist developing nations by helping to train the management, the technocracy, the leadership who will be competent to shape a nation's future. Obviously, to do this job there must be desire on the part of the multinational corporation. That desire generally does not come from threats but rather from incentives. It may well be that the multinational corporation, the Canadian banks in the Commonwealth Caribbean, should be compensated,on the basis of their developing both local business and local people. In such an effort there is much room for enlightened support from the governments of both the Commonwealth Caribbean and Canada. Drucker writes:

> The most effective agent of rapid human development in
> the economy has been the multinational corporation. . . .
> In fact we should base the activities of the multinational
> business in the developing countries less on capital in-
> vestment and ownership control than on management. The
> multinational company should get paid—and paid exceed-
> ingly well—for developing both local business and local
> people. It might not be a bad idea to make a stake in
> ownership a reward for successfully developing human
> resources in the local community—thus both giving an
> incentive to the foreign company to speed the development
> of local nationals for leadership and making sure that they
> are truly prepared for responsibility for the business.[76]

NOTES

1. West Indies and Caribbean Year Book 1972 [Barbados] (Andover, Hants, England: IPC Business Press Information Services, 1971), pp. 81, 89.
2. William G. Demas, The Economics of Development in Small Countries with Special Reference to the Caribbean (Montreal: McGill University Press, 1965), pp. 114-115.
3. The figures are astonishing, particularly for the smaller islands. Data used in this summary come from the Quarterly Reports of the Eastern Caribbean Currency Authority for the period ending September 1971 (Barbados: Research Department). Three of the smaller islands are used, namely, Antigua, Grenada, and St. Lucia.

Without exception, for each island loans have almost equaled all deposits. Without exception, for each island the largest loan categories have been those made as personal loans or those to the distributive trades. Indeed, these loans have accounted for nearly half of all loans made. The next largest category of loans have been "other," a rather general label often used to disguise loans made to local governments.

4. Levitt and McIntyre, Canada-West Indies Economic Relations (Montreal: McGill University, 1967), p. 61.

5. Ibid.

6. Ibid., p. 62.

7. Ibid., pp. 62-63.

8. H. Zinder and Associates, Inc., "The Future of Tourism in The Eastern Caribbean," a report to the Agency for International Development (Washington, D.C., May 1969).

9. Time (Canada ed.), September 18, 1972, p. 29.

10. Zinder, op. cit., p. 49.

11. Ibid., p. 50-54.

12. Ibid., pp. 207-210.

13. Ibid., p. 211.

14. Interview with the Minister of Finance in Grenada, 1971.

15. Levitt and McIntyre, op. cit., p. 62.

16. Zinder, op. cit., p. 267.

17. Ibid., p. 271.

18. Final Report of the Canadian Senate Foreign Affairs Committee Respecting the Caribbean Area, First and Second Session, 28th Parliament, 1970, 12:19.

19. Ibid. (Proceedings of the Committee), 7:42.

20. Ibid., 12:20.

21. Ibid., 12:23.

22. Horace Sutton, "The Palm Tree Revolt," Saturday Review, February 27, 1971, p. 36. Sutton points out that Hill likes to wrap these sweeping social reforms in African bunting. He decries the concept of illegitimacy (80 percent of the Jamaican population is said to be born out of formal wedlock) as a "Euroracist category of validity" and calls for a recognition of African roots of the mating pattern, family structure, and the kinship system, all with a New World Adaptation.

23. Ibid.

24. Final Report, op. cit., 7:40.

25. Ibid.

26. Toronto Globe and Mail, September 16, 1972, p. 13.

27. Final Report, op. cit., 7:40.

28. Canadian Annual Review for 1970 (Toronto: University of Toronto Press, 1971), pp. 355-356.

29. Address of Donald Fleming, Q.C., before the Nassau Chamber of Commerce, January 1972, p. 18 (mimeographed).

30. Franklin H. Wilson, "The Bahamian and Business," The Bahamas People, March 4, 1972, p. 4.

31. Levitt and McIntyre, op. cit., p. 130.

32. Ibid., p. 132.

33. Demas, op. cit., p. 149.

34. Final Report, op. cit., 12:24.

35. Ibid., 12:20.

36. For a general description of Carifta, see West Indies and Caribbean Year Book 1972, op. cit., p. ix.

37. "The Caribbean Development Bank," (Barbados: The Bank, 1971), p. 1.

38. "Financial Policies," (Barbados: Caribbean Development Bank, 1971) p. 1.

39. "CDB Press Release No. 8/71," October 27, 1971, Barbados.

40. "Canada and The Developing World" (Ottawa: CIDA, 1971), p. 18.

41. W. M. Dobell, "The Canadian Government and International Development," in R. D. H. Sallery et al., eds., Readings in Development (Ottawa: Canadian University Service Overseas, 1971), p. 88.

42. West Indies and Caribbean Year Book 1972, op. cit., p. xx.

43. QER: The West Indies, Bahamas, Bermuda, British Honduras, Guyana, No. 1-1972 (London: The Economist Intelligence Unit, 1972), p. 11.

44. Ibid, p. 3.

45. Levitt and McIntyre, op. cit., pp. 115-116.

46. "CIDA: Commonwealth Caribbean Assistance Program" (Ottawa: CIDA), p. 4.

47. Ibid., p. 7.

48. Ibid., p. 15.

49. Ibid., p. 11.

50. Ibid., p. 12.

51. "CIDA Annual Review, 1969" (Ottawa: CIDA, 1970), pp. 28, 40.

52. Final Report, op. cit., 12:27.

53. Third Five-Year Plan, 1969-1973, Government of Trinidad and Tobago as Approved by Parliament (Trinidad: Government Printery, 1970), pp. 268-275.

54. Ibid., p. 266.

55. Demas, op. cit., p. 98.

56. Ibid.

57. Ibid., p. 99.

58. Third Five-Year Plan, op. cit., p. 270.

59. Ibid., p. 274.

60. Ibid., p. 275.

61. Ibid.

62. Ibid.

63. Final Report, op. cit., 12:70.

64. John M. Culbertson, Economic Development: An Ecological Approach (New York: Alfred A. Knopf, 1971), pp. 167-168.

65. Ibid., pp. 168-169.

66. Ibid., p. 170.

67. Fleming, op. cit., pp. 8-10.

68. Final Report, op. cit., 12:70.

69. International Development: Foreign Policy for Canadians (Ottawa: Information Canada, 1970), p. 21.

70. "Canada and the Developing World, 1970-71," (Ottawa: CIDA, 1971).

71. Ibid.

72. "CIDA Annual Review, 1969," op. cit., p. 47.

73. "Canada and the Developing World, 1970-71," op. cit.

74. Ibid.

75. Peter F. Drucker, The Age of Discontinuity: Guidelines to Our Changing Society (New York: Harper and Row, 1968), pp. 129-130.

76. Ibid., p. 130.

CHAPTER

7

CANADA'S BANKS:
AN INSTRUMENT OF
ECONOMIC NATIONALISM

Canada's banks in Commonwealth Caribbean are global corporations; their operations are of great concern to the area's mini-states. Yet it remains a somewhat curious fact that Canada's external policy for the Commonwealth Caribbean is formulated and implemented as if the Canadian global corporations do not exist. Canada has the power to compel its banks to a given course of action. Canada can, if it so desires, force its banks to conduct themselves as "good corporate citizens" in developing nations. Indeed, Canada can even work together with its banks to achieve positive foreign aid goals.

One rationale for Canada's non-action toward its own banks might rest on a "free enterprise" base. That is, Canada is a "free enterprise" state. Its banks are private businesses. Except for monetary policy it is not the function of government to regulate the private sector of banking. Moreover, for Canada to regulate banking in the Commonwealth Caribbean would be an improper interference in the internal affairs of another sovereign state. Thus, private enterprise and sovereignty can serve as grounds for Canadian non-action against its own global corporations.

Is that rationale valid? In a real sense that is the question probed in this chapter. The search for an answer may rest in Canada's own reaction to the global corporations of other nation-states doing business in Canada. Is Canada able to look into a mirror and require less of its global corporations than is demanded of those foreign enterprises operating in Canada? The facts seem to indicate that Canada applies a dual standard: Good corporate citizenship is expected of those foreign multinational enterprises doing business in Canada. Good corporate citizenship is not required even of those state-endorsed Canadian multinational enterprises doing business outside of Canada.

This chapter will demonstrate that Canada clearly views the foreign multinational corporation as a potential threat to its sovereignty.

136

Because of its concern Canada has developed a three-pronged approach with one overriding goal, Canadianization of global enterprises occupying significant positions in essential industries. The three-pronged approach permits (1) screening investments; (2) Canadian participation either in the investments or in the direction of the enterprise; (3) Canadian ownership of the enterprise.

Canada has reserved, with only very limited exception, both ownership and control of its banks to Canadian citizens. Moreover, government has become directly involved in banking operations through the Bank Act, the chartering instrument for banks, and the Bank of Canada, a powerful regulating authority. More than any other endeavor the banking industry has been singled out as essential to the economy. It has been thoroughly Canadianized. It has been made powerful in world terms. It has been both regulated and shielded by the government.

As a matter of enlightened foreign policy why shouldn't Canada encourage precisely the same policy for Canadian banks operating in the Commonwealth Caribbean? Why shouldn't Canada use its power and its purse to assist in the conversion of Canadian banks to Caribbean banks? Only the Senate of Canada has addressed itself to the achievement of such a policy. But the Senate lacks the power of the House of Commons; it does not speak for the government.

Could it be that a narrower, more traditional view of enlightened foreign policy is at play? Could it be that that policy is best which furthers Canada's own economic interests? Whatever, within reason, furthers the maximization of Canadian banking profits outside of Canada is in the interest of the Canadian government. Is this the proposition that directly or indirectly influences Canada's external policy? This chapter probes Canada's approach to the global corporation. In so doing there may come more insight into Canada's external policy toward the Commonwealth Caribbean.

CANADIAN RESPONSE TO THE "AMERICAN
CHALLENGE": LESSONS FOR THE
COMMONWEALTH CARIBBEAN?

In 1968 the Liberal Party of Canada under the leadership of Pierre Trudeau swept to power by a commanding majority. In the fall of 1972 that party again faced the electorate. For some, including the socialist-oriented New Democratic Party, which held a poor third position in the Federal House of Commons behind the official opposition party of the Progressive Conservatives, foreign control over the Canadian economy was a major campaign issue. For Prime Minister Trudeau foreign control was not the kind of issue that merited a massive frontal attack by the government. Rather, he told the electorate that his government, his party, strove for consistency in the protection of identifiable Canadian interests. It was not his concern simply to strike at the United States. The Prime Minister said:

> If it is totally wrong under all circumstances, say, for
> Wall Street to dominate Canada's economy, then it must
> be totally wrong for Bay Street [in Toronto] to dominate
> Quebec's economy. . . . [The Canadian independence the
> Government is defending] is not just concerned with for-
> eign investment. It is directed as much to our territorial
> integrity as it is to our financial institutions. It is as
> much directed to our cultural expression as to our indus-
> trial development. . . . The ends we all seek will elude
> us if we so focus our energies and our emotions on merely
> one aspect of the Canadian entity . . . that we lose all
> balance and all proportion.[1]

A month after the Prime Minister spoke the election was held. The Liberal Party lost its majority; the Progressive Conservatives held about an equal number of seats with the Liberals. And the New Democrats held the balance of power with thirty-one seats. Like the New Democrats, the Progressive Conservatives were sensitive to the foreign and largely American multinational corporation and its "penetration" of the Canadian economy. In what were called major policy statements, the Progressive Censervatives spoke to the issue of foreign ownership. Their emphasis was not so much on economic independence as on profitable trading arrangements, but the difference was only one of degree: Concern was expressed that Canada not be excluded from the emerging world trading blocs. "Other factors clouding the Canadian trade picture are the presence in Canada of substantial numbers of multinational corporations which, in some instances, retard Canada's ability to make its own decisions and to develop its own technology for world markets."[2] The remedies suggested were:[3]

    1. Bring the multinational enterprise under Federal jurisdiction.

    2. Require full financial disclosure from Canadian-based subsidiaries of the foreign-based corporations.

    3. Require that the Canadian-based subsidiaries have a majority of resident Canadians on their boards "so that the operation of these companies will reflect a first-hand knowledge of Canadian conditions and be sensitive to Canadian interests and considerations. In addition measures would be implemented to ensure that executive officers are also Canadians."

    4. Insure that foreign-owned companies operating in Canada are not susceptible to parent country laws and regulations which may be in conflict with Canadian interests.

Post-election public opinion polls indicated that economic independence was not a major issue to the voters; they were disturbed more fundamentally by rising inflation and unemployment. Nevertheless, the New Democrats and the Progressive Conservatives did make an issue of foreign ownership. And Prime Minister Trudeau in forming a minority government had not forgotten that fact.

THE WATKINS REPORT OF 1968

To understand the origin of the "felt" problem for the global corporation in 1972, we go back only a few years. It was in January 1968 that Canadian attention focused specifically upon the global corporation; only then did that concern rise to a quasi-governmental level with the report "Foreign Ownership and the Structure of Canadian Industry" (Watkins Report), prepared for the Privy Council Office. Initiated by Walter Gordon, the controversial Minister of Finance and later President of the Privy Council, the Watkins Report was prepared exclusively by academics. Guided by economists and political economists, it attempted to view the global corporation through the eyes of the nation-state. First came a statement of issues and national goals:

> The multinational corporation is a growing feature of the
> embryonic world economy. Many industries, including
> those based on the new technologies, are characterized
> by large corporations whose operations span the globe.
> This international business integration adds new dimen-
> sions to national policies. Canadians are concerned that
> these corporations be truly multinational, genuinely re-
> specting Canadian aspirations, and that Canada's national
> policies ensure that their behavior is fully consistent
> with Canadian goals . . . Two of the goals uppermost in
> the minds of Canadians today are national independence
> and a rising standard of living.[4]

Setting forth the structure of Canadian industry, economists and political economists asked how national independence could be achieved while at the same time the nation pursued a higher standard of living. They asked the question because they found that much of Canadian industry is controlled by subsidiaries of American corporations. Long-term foreign investments in Canada rose from $7 billion (U.S.) in 1945 to $27 billion (U.S.) in 1964. Direct investment such as plant construction or company absorption grew from $2.7 billion (U.S.) in 1945 to $15.9 billion (U.S.) in 1964, of which the United States accounted for 80 percent or $12.9 billion (U.S.).[5] (The United Kingdom holds the second position, with 12 percent of the total.) In addition, United States ownership is increasing rather than decreasing and is centered in industries vital to the Canadian economy. Relatively few American firms held 97 percent of the auto manufacturing and parts market, 90 percent of the rubber market, 54 percent of the chemical market, and 66 percent of the electrical apparatus market.[6]

The Watkins Report also lists some of the elements that go to make the American corporation successful: technological leadership, brand names, entrepreneurial drive, favorable tax policy, and finally, "the tendency of some American firms to regard Canada as not a foreign country hastened and strengthened penetration into Canada."[7]

What are the economic costs of American penetration? Before entering this discussion the Watkins Report makes it very clear that a free trade policy rather than high tariffs might have inhibited American corporations from establishing branch plants and exposed Canadia enterprise to the winds of competition. This was not done and America corporations came to the Canadian market through a back door. For Canada the experience has been debilitating. Listen to the summary bill of particulars: (1) The Canadian capital market has not developed the capacity to mobilize risk capital, which is essential for large resource development. The development of the Canadian capital marke and accumulation of Canadian equities has been inhibited by the prevalence of the wholly-owned subsidiary, which does not issue its shares to Canadians. (2) The use of American management, particularly at the top echelon, tends to weaken both the capacity and the pressure on Canadians to fill the same positions. This is reflected in the quality of Canadian education. (3) Government assistance for industrial research and development has slackened relative to other developed countries. In part, this is attributed to the fact that the American corporation provides the technological development which Canada would otherwise be forced to find itself.[8]

The sum total of the economic liabilities is dependence through economic integration, a fact of which the United States is not unaware. It is at this point that the Watkins Report reaches the nub of the matter: The economic power of the American-based global corporation gives the United States government the opportunity to carry forwai foreign policy, thereby giving American law the capacity for extraterritorial application. The Watkins Report is specific; it categorizes the subjects of intrusion: American-owned subsidiaries subject to American law and policy on freedom to export; United States antitrust law and policy; and United States balance of payments policy.[9]

There were data enough to support the rather obvious impact of American industry in Canada. There was but minimal information recited to support the conclusions relating to the economic costs of

American influence. It is worth noting the major concessions made by the Watkins Report: (1) Foreign-owned subsidiaries perform as well as Canadian-owned firms, but distinctly worse than the foreign firms. The environment within which firms operate is more relevant than nationality for many aspects of their performance.[10] (2) Subsidiaries perform either as well as or better than Canadian-owned firms in research and development.[11] (3) Relative to investment and gross national product, American-based corporations are not simply extracting their profits through dividends. Though dividends to foreigners have risen to $1 billion (U.S.) annually, expressed as a percentage of gross national product they have fallen from 2.9 percent in the late 1920s and 6.4 percent in the 1930s to 1.9 percent from 1957 through 1965.[12]

In the final analysis the report took the view that if the nation-state is to survive it must have coherence and unity of its various spheres. The penetration or disruption of any one sphere by an outside force, whether it be political, legal, economic, or any other, produces inevitable ramifications in other spheres.[13] The problem as put by the report is one of control, involving the capacity of a nation-state to shape its own means and ends. The solution, agreed to by all members of the Task Force, was twofold: free the multinational corporation of intervention by foreign government, and give Canadian presence to the multinational corporation doing business in Canada.[14]

The "solutions" sought by the Watkins Task Force are not unlike the "solutions" sought by nations in the Commonwealth Caribbean. It is fair to say that Canada has not opposed those solutions. Canada, as such, has not used its banks to intervene in the internal affairs of other nation-states. Nor has Canada opposed the "Caribbeanization" of its banks. Yet the fact remains that the "solutions" deemed adequate for Canada by the Watkins Task Force do not fully suit the needs of the Commonwealth Caribbean. More than the psychological placebo of perceived Caribbean government control over banks is needed. The Commonwealth Caribbean as a developing area proximate to affluent North America must muster its resources for development. Bank deposits are a major national resource. Sovereignty over banks should mean that deposit funds can be used as the nation-state dictates. Reality is harsh for many of the Commonwealth Caribbean nation-states. The fact of sovereignty will not always bring the resources of the banks into play as governments might desire.

Consider the legal instruments of control and their limitations: Equity participation is not likely to be successful except for the more populous and developed islands of Jamaica, Trinidad and Tobago, and Barbados. Even then needed capital will be diverted from other enterprises to banking. Control over bank directorships may lend a national presence to the banks, but not necessarily bring a change in investment policy. That is, so long as a bank remains a private enterprise it must operate on a profit-maximization principle. It cannot use its capital or deposit moneys in unproductive ways. This is especially true for a bank. Unproductive utilization of funds can quickly bring depositor mistrust and a withdrawal of deposits, the lifeblood for investments. So, too, central bank legislation can succeed only to a point. Any major diversion of deposit moneys to unproductive uses can bring prompt depositor reaction, particularly if the island-nation is small in population and limited in resources. In such a setting the communications chain moves with great speed.

CANADIAN COMPETITION FOR GLOBAL ENTERPRISES

The Watkins Report was prepared under the direction of a forme Liberal Minister of Finance, whose budget and policy proved embarrassing to his party. Professor Watkins found a national platform through the report. He organized supporters for political action against "economic imperialism" and for "economic socialism." His supporters sought to work their will not in the Liberal party, but in the New Democratic Party. Indeed, they became a major force within the NDP. They formally organized themselves as the "Waffle Wing" within the NDP and issued what they called the "Waffle Manifesto." They succeeded in placing some of their members on the executive councils at both the provincial and federal levels. They succeeded in having some of their members nominated to run for political office in various riding associations or political wards. In all these matters they held themselves out as the Waffle Wing of the NDP. As such, they were a divisive force, and they became even more divisive in their support of an independent Quebec. The party majority reacted and challenged the Wafflers with an ultimatum: Either become part of the party and dissolve the Waffle Wing as such, or be read out of the party. Some, including Professor Watkins, left the NDP, and othe accepted the ultimatum. The Waffle Wing was dissolved.

Yet the force that the Wafflers unleashed had its effect on all the major parties. Each attempted in its own way to defuse the issue of economic nationalism. Each attempted to absorb and resolve the issues of economic nationalism within an already existing party and governmental structure. None of the three major parties wanted change that could be equivalent to social and economic revolution.

The Watkins Report was completed and published during the early days of the Liberal Party's great 1968 majority rule of the federal government. For more than two years the Liberal governmer resisted any formal response to the report. By 1970, however, Canar as a nation was caught in an economic vise of inflation and rising

142

unemployment far in excess of that in the United States. For the federal government the problem was made even more difficult as the nation's largest trading partner, the United States, began to assert itself and, among other things, lure American corporations back to their home country with promises of tax concessions. At the same time the American government initiated a sharp review of Canada's most-favored-nation status.

Under Minister Without Portfolio Herb Gray, former chairman of the House of Commons Finance Committee, responsibility was assigned in the spring of 1970 to bring forward proposals on foreign investment policy. For nearly two years Gray labored while the press speculated. Then in December 1971, The Canadian Forum, an intellectual magazine with a small circulation under the editorship of a former member of the Watkins task force, obtained what purported to be an unauthorized copy of the Gray Report.[15] It was published as a full issue of the magazine. The government responded by denying that the document represented official government policy, and, at the same time, it initiated investigations to determine responsibility for "leaking" the document.

Several months later the government published a modified "Gray Report," titled Foreign Direct Investment in Canada. In the foreword to the report the government stated that it was being published to help public understanding. "The document, while being published under the authority of the Government of Canada, is not a statement of government policy nor should it be assumed that the government endorses all aspects of the analysis contained in it."[16]

It is worth noting that the government modified some significant points in the Gray Report before agreeing to publication. Yet it refused to hold the report out as official policy. The end result was to present to the public, and, it must be added, the American government, a frame of reference and an interpretation of the meaning of foreign ownership in Canada.

The government's report did not unduly upset the Canadian or American business community. The general business reaction was that the report allowed business to continue and to be productive without major government restraints. The single major thrust of the government was the establishment of a screening board with wide-ranging powers over foreign investment. The board would be vested with significant discretion to bargain with foreign-based industry to achieve the best possible results for Canada. For the extracting industries this might mean the establishment of refining and processing plants in Canada rather than shipment of raw ores abroad. For manufacturing companies, the screening board might demand that a share of technological research take place in Canada and that meaningful Canadian managerial talent be employed.[17]

The Gray Report was driving toward maximization of benefits to Canada from foreign ownership. Except for so-called culture-based industries such as broadcasting companies where firms were to be Canadian controlled, negotiations with the review board would focus upon specific criteria designed to achieve economic goals.[18] Social values, on the whole, were not to play any role in screening board negotiations. The report stated:

> There is a danger that a review process would become an instrument for the implementation of a variety of government policies and programmes unrelated to the objectives of the review process. For instance, pressures could develop to block a particular foreign investment unless certain anti-pollution steps are taken. This risk would be minimized if a review process is guided strictly by its own criteria in making decisions with other considerations being dealt with by other arms of the government.[19]

Despite Canada's broad discretion to make economic decisions the global corporation operating in Canada is not slated to lose, although the corporation's home government might lose. The Gray Report clearly wants to make the corporation successful in Canada. For the American-based global corporation this might mean closing plants in the United States in order to expand in Canada, but the costs might be more than offset by benefits. There might be a loss to the American economy, but that is of no direct concern to the global corporation concerned with global profits. Indeed, a properly functioning screening committee might even assist the foreign corporation in Canada to become dominant, superior to the domestic Canadian corporation. Thus the Gray Report noted:

> If a review process alone were implemented, and nothing were done to improve the industrial capacities of Canadian entrepreneurs, the result might be a relative increase in efficiency in the foreign controlled sector. The degree of foreign control of Canadian business might, therefore, continue to increase to the extent that foreign investors were willing to meet the standards set by the review agency.[20]

The foreign multinational enterprise is in Canada, and its influence is real. The Gray Report does not propose to eliminate but rather to Canadianize that influence. What better source could there be for breeding the Canadian global corporation than through the foreign global corporation conducting massive operations in

Canada? Such Canadian global corporations would be encouraged by government where internationalization is occuring and where Canada has a comparative advantage.

> The alternative would be to have more foreign branch
> plants of multinational companies operating in Canada in
> these industries, or to shut out multinationals altogether,
> thereby denying Canada the efficiencies which multina-
> tional corporations can generate in some cases, such as
> lower costs, increased competition and greater tech-
> nological development. . . . It is more likely that a Cana-
> dian controlled firm, including a Canadian based MNE
> [multinational enterprise], will tend to more bias toward
> locating activity in Canada than will a foreign controlled
> firm, which can be helpful in rooting technology and pro-
> duction in this country.21

Once established, the very size and scope of a global corporation, now flying a Canadian flag, can be expected to be a lure to bright young Canadian managers and scientists. By definition the global corporation will offer opportunities far beyond Canada's borders and it will afford the resources both human and material to see a goal accomplished. It is the intent of the Gray Report to establish the Canadian global corporation as an institution. As such it can be expected to stand against both individual and corporate pressures. That is, individuals will have both good and bad effects on the enterprise, but it will be hardly likely that the enterprise will fail because of any one person. Similarly, because of its very size, the enterprise will not be readily amenable to other corporate takeover. Indeed, its size, and the self-savings (that is, retained earnings) of the global corporation place it in a favorable position to take over other businesses. In sum, Canada seems to be opting for an institution capable of sustaining itself indefinitely, thereby affording domestic protection against foreign economic penetration.

Once established, the global corporation flying a Canadian flag might not be subject to the restraints imposed upon the foreign corporation in Canada. The Gray Report seemed to accept on balance a belief that the Canadian global corporation, while subject to many of the same drives as other global corporations, would have a Canadian bias. Moreover, the report seemed to shy away from any act that might cause the Canadian global enterprise to shift domicile:

> Reviewing Canadian MNEs [by the proposed screening
> board] would involve scrutinizing the entire operations of

these firms including the activities of all their foreign
subsidiaries. Reviewing foreign controlled firms would,
by contrast, involve looking primarily at only one branch
of the foreign MNEs operations, thus subjecting Canadian
MNEs to a wider review that a foreign owned firm. Therefore, subjected to this greater degree of review, it is
likely that a high proportion of Canadian multinational
enterprises would locate their headquarters elsewhere,
with Canada losing those benefits associated with having
the headquarters in this country.[22]

In summary, therefore, the following appears to be one line of
attack against foreign economic penetration as posited by the Gray
Report: Establish a screening board over all foreign investment.
Give that board power to maximize Canadian economic benefits and
minimize Canadian economic costs flowing from foreign investment.
Let the board in its bargaining process and the government by other
action be supportive of Canadian global enterprises. Recognize that
a Canadian global enterprise should have an economic bias favorable
to Canada, and, as such, should provide an institutional outlet for
Canadian managerial and research talent. Finally, do not·place the
Canadian global enterprise in a less favorable position than a foreign
business in Canada. To do so would be to cause the Canadian company
to shift domicile.
    The Gray Report is designed to further Canadian economic
interests. As finally published the Gray Report evidences a single
concern solely for Canada. It is not concerned with the effect of Canadian economic nationalism on other nations. This is made clear in
the difference between the first, "unauthorized," text of the report
and the final, "authorized," text. The first draft warned:

> Ministers should note that a policy to encourage the devel-
> opment of Canadian MNEs, at least in certain sectors, will
> affect the scope of any international initiatives the Govern-
> ment may wish to take to control the growth and power of
> the MNEs in general. It would be difficult for the Govern-
> ment to launch an international initiative to control the
> powers of the MNE and at the same time implement
> policies to develop MNEs.[23]

Despite this warning, the first report came to the same conclusion as the final report: The Canadian global enterprise should be
encouraged under certain circumstances. What was omitted from the
second report was the warning that Canadian international initiatives
would have to be restrained, that they could no longer be addressed

to the power of the global enterprise, that they could no longer solicit international, multistate efforts to control and harness their power to serve a broader social and economic interest, one that would transcend national boundaries.

As an affluent and powerful nation in its own right Canada, in the Gray Report, was looking only to its own interests. Its perspective on the global corporation was quite narrow, as can be seen in the section on international initiatives—in a report covering 523 pages, only four pages are devoted to the theme. The action Canada might take is confined to achieving the integrity of national jurisdiction. That is, international cooperation should focus upon each nation being able to make its laws operate on the global enterprise doing business in that nation. The Gray Report suggested that a code might contain the following provisions:

1. Recognition by home governments that their national firms are not to be used as a vehicle for extension of their laws into foreign countries.

2. The obligation of host countries to act in a fair and equitable manner toward foreign investment.

3. Renunciation by a government which itself engages in foreign direct investment of any special status for that investment merely because it was one made by government.

4. Providing Most Favored Nation treatment to foreign investors, rather than national treatment. This would guarantee that all foreign investors would be treated alike.

5. Recognition of the right of host countries to fix rules to ensure adequate domestic control of their economies.[24]

Nothing is said in the Gray Report of those nations, such as some in the Commonwealth Caribbean, so weak and so dominated by foreign global corporations that they are unable to shape their own economic destiny. Canada is not such a weak nation; it can shape its own destiny. It would like international cooperation that would be supportive of such efforts; it feels under no particular responsibility to aid in fashioning an international code to protect the weak.

The rationale behind Canada's position may afford some insight into the perception of power by the nation-state: The global corporation in Canada in 1972 is largely foreign controlled. It constitutes a challenge to the government itself. The government responds to the challenge by regulating the foreign enterprise and assisting the establishment of domestic enterprises over which it has some meaningful control. By such acts the government preserves its own integrity and its own capacity to act in response to the electorate. Yet in taking such actions, the government may well encroach upon the powers of other nation-states that find themselves penetrated and dominated not merely by American, or Common Market, or Japanese, but also by Canadian global enterprises.

The Watkins Report and the Gray Report are not documents addressed to achieving a greater morality. Rather, they are argument designed to bring a strengthened economic nationalism. Both reports make it clear that Canada will compete in the development of multinational enterprises. Banks are among Canada's most important global corporations. There appears to be an answer to one question posed at the beginning of this chapter: Canada is not likely to embark on a foreign policy that is directed toward the destruction of its own globa enterprises.

NATIONALISM AND BUSINESS RATIONALITY

In one sense the issue for Canada properly may be: What, if anything, can be done to assist the Commonwealth Caribbean to achiev the real objective of economic growth? Canada's banks as global enterprises need not be hurtful; they can even be supportive of proper development in the area. After all, as global corporations, like most profit-motivated enterprises, they will attempt to adjust to the demand of nationalism. Equity participation of nationals can be allowed so long as the business continues to yield a reasonable profit. A preferential employment system for nationals can be initiated so long as the business maintains relative efficiency. Capital plant construction and research expansion can take place so long as there is some likelihood of return to the business. Within limits, within the tolerances of the marketplace, business can respond to the pressures of nationalism.

A key issue relates not so much to the tolerance level of busines but to the force level of nationalism. In a very real sense business operates at the will of government. That is, government has the power, both in law and in fact, to eliminate any business operation. This power is not made less real by the importance of the business to the economy. The Asian community in Uganda might have been the backbone of much of that country's economy. That did not stop the government from forcibly deporting the entire Asian community, and, by doing so, eliminating a substantial sector of business.

In the same way as the Asian community in Uganda was expelled the global corporation, despite its worldwide asset position, is vulnerable to nationalist attack. As such, neither the global worth of the corporation nor its importance to any particular nation-state economy may shield the enterprise from nationalist demands. The global enterprise is not a challenge to the nation-state. Sir Isaiah Berlin, President of Wolfson College, Oxford, writes:

Faith in countervailing forces—in multinational corporations which, whatever their relationship with class war and social conflict, at any rate do cross national borders, or in the United Nations as a barrier to unbridled chauvinism—seems about as realistic (at least so far as lands outside Western Europe are concerned) as Cobden's belief that the development of free trade throughout the world would of itself ensure peace and harmonious cooperation between nations. One is also reminded of Norman Angell's apparently unanswered argument a short while before 1914 that the economic interests of modern capitalist states alone made large-scale wars impossible.[25]

The point to be made is that nationalism can act against the self-interest of the citizenry. That is, Uganda could expel its Asian population and Germany destroy its Jewish citizens, but such nationalism demands an economic price as well as a moral one. Today a central question is just what the nature of nationalism is.

None can question the rise of nationalism in the 1960s and 1970s. In newly developed states it often is the single important factor. And, indeed, it is often the single most important factor for a revolutionary movement whether it be in Ireland, Bangladesh, Biafra, Uganda, or even French Canada. What one must ask is why nationalism has achieved such dominance. Berlin offers a partial answer:

In most of these cases the desire for national independence is intertwined with social resistance to exploitation. This kind of nationalism is, perhaps, as much a form of social or class resistance as of purely national self-assertion, creating a mood in which men prefer to be ordered about, even if this entails ill-treatment, by members of their own faith or nation or class to tutelage, however benevolent, on the part of ultimately patronizing superiors from a foreign land or alien class or milieu.[26]

Yet one wonders why people might prefer greater hardship administered by fellow-nationals as against greater material well-being from foreigners. Why should General Amin of Uganda have been applauded by his countrymen for expelling the Asian community which formed a part of that country's economic life? The rationale given by the general was that the Asians were not part of the country; they had chosen to isolate themselves, to become an elite who would not integrate with the black majority. What the general seemed to be saying is that the Asians, while Ugandan citizens, should be treated

149

as foreigners, even hostile foreigners, for they did not integrate themselves into the whole community.

Surely on the face of it the passionate nationalism of Uganda bears scant relationship to 19th century nationalism, which minimized the importance of race, nationality, and even culture as opposed to class or economic competition. Nineteenth-century nationalism made basic assumptions based upon either liberal individualism or technocratic centralization. The key to either assumption, however, was rooted in nationalism. Humanity ultimately would act in its own best interests, and it would follow that nationalism with its national boundaries would fall as history and humanity marched toward a single, progressive, universal civilization.[27] Such, too, was Marxist doctrine. Applied, it would have caused an end to World War I, for the workers of the world simply would not have supported the war effort. Applied, it would have stopped the Hungarian revolution of 1956, the rise of Polish nationalism with its attendant anti-Semitism at the same time, and, as well, the same growth of nationalism and race consciousness within the Soviet Union itself.

Nationalism is rampant in the 20th century, but the nationalism of the 19th century seems inapplicable. There is in the new nationalism in the opinion of Sir Isaiah Berlin, a rejection of rationalist solution to human problems. Carried to its logical conclusion the rationalist approach places primary reliance on science, and this in turn means an objectification of needs and solutions. The rationalist approach finds expression in systems analysis and cost effectiveness. It finds its implementation in a technocracy which might even include Stalin's "engineers of human souls."

The rationalist approach has been the vehicle for effecting the industrial and even postindustrial or cerebral society. It is used by all large-scale economic and even cultural activities conducted by government, capitalist and communist, as well as business enterprises.

> It is against this [rationalist approach] that a worldwide protest has begun. . . . It springs from the feeling that human rights, rooted in the sense of human beings as specifically human, that is, as individuated, as possessing wills, sentiments, beliefs, ideals, wages of living of their own, have been lost sight of in the "global" calculations and vast extrapolations which guide the plans of policy planners and executives in the gigantic operations in which governments, corporations, elites of various kinds are engaged. Quantitative computation cannot but ignore the specific wishes and hopes and fears and goals of individual human beings.[28]

Planning for efficiency, for productivity, is the concern of states and corporations. The better the planning, the more the individual will find a future defined, a course of conduct that will be "correct." Individual options, alternatives, will be narrowed for the state, and the corporations doing business within its boundaries will have specific needs that individuals must fill. The state and the corporation will act upon the individual; the individual will not act upon the state and the corporation. Against this the individual rebels; the human personality rejects treatment as simply human material; the benevolent motives of the state and corporate planners are of no moment.

In industrial and postindustrial societies the protest comes from individuals and groups who often reject the overriding goal of growth in the gross national product. The citizenry view their environs and ask whether the extent of material well-being is worth the price in environmental pollution. In the developing nations the demand takes the form of insisting on being treated as their former masters were treated. They want, they demand, not only the right to make their own decisions, but also the same material well-being as their former masters.

The self that seeks liberty of action, determination of its own life, can be large or small, regional or linguistic; today it is liable to be collective and national or ethnic-religious rather than individual; it is always resistant to dilution, assimilation, depersonalization. It is the very triumph of scientific rationalism everywhere, the great eighteenth-century movement for the liberation of men from superstitution and ignorance, from the selfishness and greed of kings, priests, and oligarchies, above all, from the vagaries of natural forces, that, by a curious paradox, has imposed a yoke that, in its turn, evoked an all-too-human cry for independence from its rule. It is a cry for room in which men can seek to realize their natures, quirks and all, to live lives free from dictation or coercion from teachers, masters, bullies and persuaders and dominators of various kinds. No doubt to do entirely as one likes could destroy not only one's neighbors but oneself. Freedom is only one value among others, and cannot be realized without rules and limits. But in the hour of revolt this is inevitably forgotten.[29]

From all that has been said comes a rather curious conclusion: It is the state and the corporation which it tolerates that impose an overburdening nationalism and attendant technocracy on the populace.

151

Yet the populace look to the state with their "new" nationalism to throw off the political and business yoke. Why? If the state is an institutional source of wrong, should it not be dissolved and a new structure created under which humanity could live? Do we answer the question amply by asking "Do we look to the state because the state is present? I think not. We have made the concept of the state a needs-satisfying body for its citizens. The state, by itself or together with institutionalized religion, can allow for the transfer, the displacement of childhood emotions, of problems and tensions, from parents to the state. The child transfers a part of his feeling to the state in the hope and belief of a spiritually nourishing national life:

> The ego protects itself against what would be a depressing self-realization of continuing immaturity by projecting the yearning for the mother into the nation image, making animate and gratuitously fulfilling an otherwise abstract entity. The childish boast "my mother is better than yours" becomes "my country right or wrong" in the adult. The venerating idealization of the national leader results from the transference of feelings to him that were, in the beginning, fixed upon the father. When these feelings are inadequately neutralized the original ambivalent feelings of living awe and jealous hatred toward the father are retained in the transference. The idealization of the remote, powerful figure of the leader is a defence against the destructive side of the ambivalence in the led, just as the passionate striving for power and prestige in the leader is often an attempt to overcome and deny his anxiety.[30]

By such means the nation becomes in the unconscious emotional mind a superfamily. As such, as an artificial family, the nation takes up the burden of resolving individual emotional conflicts left unresolved by the natural family. A bond of brotherhood is developed. For many the British monarchy as a mother figure becomes a necessity.[31] For many, too, there is an obligation to test filial loyalty by a call to arms.

War, hostility, and aggression are necessary factors in nationalism. A psychiatrist might offer the following rationale in support of the statement made: Nationalism can make a nation a superfamily who then becomes vested with the duty of solving individual problems. Reality dictates that not all of those problems, those felt tensions, will be resolved. Yet it is the individual himself who has acquiesced in nationalism; his ego will not easily let him criticize himself or the new mother figure he created. Blame for the failure to resolve his problems, or those of the superfamily, will be transferred to those outside the superfamily. Indeed, blame will be transferred even if facts have to be invented.[32]

SUMMARY

When problems arise, fault is found not within the superfamily but without, for the family must be seen as strong. Thus, failure on the part of Canada to find its own independent place within the family of nations comes in no small measure from American intrusion in the Canadian economy. Reassurance by the President that the United States has no intention of wishing Canada other than a fully independent life is really an expression of American domination.[33] If only Canada could assert control over its own economy the nation would be able to find itself; internal problems of dissension would wither and die.

For the nationalist Canadian the United States must be rejected. The Viet Nam War becomes only another element of proof of the decadence of American society. The American global corporation becomes a tool of the American government. This need to reject the United States is further emphasized by the fact that the United States with its larger population and present greater wealth has all the vestige of nationhood. It has revolutionary war heroes. It has a constitution of its own, and one that does more than distribute powers between levels of government. Long before Canada it had a flag of its own making. It has a head of state whose office has the prestige of the Crown of old. In all these respects the United States differs from Canada.[34]

Canada is a nation in evolution. There are those who would still hold the nation to be British North America, the better part of the colonies that did not revolt. The reality remains, however, that Canada is a nation with two distinct cultures, French and English. That distinction is built into Canada's constitution, the British North America Act, as given by the English Parliament. Canada has a land mass greater than that of continental United States, but a population of only 21 million, most of whom live proximate to the American border. This compares with an American population of 200 million. And Canada's only continental neighbor whose territory abuts on her own is the United States.

For Canada, officially a bicultural society, and in fact a multicultural society, nationalism in the 1970s has limited channels in which to run. So long as Quebec, French Canada, forms a part of the nation then nationalism cannot find expression in the creation of a single culture; it cannot create the myth of the melting pot of peoples out of which is forged the true Canadian. This is not to say that a new

flag and a new anthem cannot be given to the people. Nor does it deny
the power of the state to command its youth to salute that flag each
school day by the singing of the anthem, and to relate religion to that
song by the recitation of a Protestant prayer. By so doing the young
are gradually born into the Canadian tribe.[35]

Yet, once in the Canadian tribe, nationalism as a cultural expression tends to lose its force. In Canada nationalism by definition
must accept multicultural expression; it cannot be used as a means
for creating a distinctive, segregated Canadian culture. At best,
nationalism can only allow opportunity for Canadians to express themselves as artists.

It is primarily in the economic area where nationalism can fully
assert itself. To protect the "integrity" of the nation, nationalism
can demand high tariffs, and it can garner individual savings in the
pursuit of larger economic ventures. It can build a transcontinental
railroad, and highways from the south to the Arctic Ocean. It should
not be forgotten that Canada came into being at the same time that
Darwinism came to the world, when industrialization transformed
European, English, and American society, and when the industrial
might of the North crushed the South in the American Civil War.

> In sum, then, the National Policy, a policy for a "Cana-
> dian economy" and a "Big Canada", a materialistic policy
> for a materialistic age, was the obvious policy to give
> expression to Canadian national sentiment. That policy
> was adopted in 1878 and accepted by the Liberal Party
> in 1896. Three years later J. I. Tarte urged Laurier to
> do more than simply accept the National Policy, to expand
> upon it with more railways, canals and harbour improve-
> ments (and presumably with higher tariffs). "Voilà",
> he observed, "le programme le plans national et de plus
> populaire que nous puissons offrir au pays."[36]

Canada, like all other countries, exhibits the character of nationalism. The only differences go to the intensity of that feeling and the
objects upon which that feeling might operate. In Canada there is in
the 1970s intense nationalism, and it is operating primarily on the
economic sector. The specific object of attack is the American global
corporation. While nationalistic arguments may have a gloss of
rationality to them, there does exist a core of irrationality: There
must be Canadian control of the Canadian economy so that a Canadian
culture might be developed. American intrusion into that economy
is equivalent to American attack on Canadian identity. Against such
an argument there is no rational response. To say that the American
global corporation is not the same as the American government will

not suffice. To remove the American corporation with its attendant loss of Canadian jobs would only go to prove the callous, unfeeling attitude of the American government.

To ask for a moderation of nationalism is fundamentally irrelevant. Being a nationalist is something that happens to a person; it is not something he chooses rationally.[37] What is needed is a constructive outlet for nationalism. The question must be asked how nationalism as such might be restrained while the state encourages the development of the individual. In the end, a democratic state should want its citizens to say, "I am a person, and I am glad to be a citizen." The state should not want the citizens to say, "Because I am a citizen of the state I am a person."

Historically the state of Canada has been concerned with economic matters in the pursuit of nationalism. In this regard Canada has embarked on grand ventures. With massive effort it constructed a transcontinental rail system. As an expression of nationalism it formed Canadian banks that rival world banks in size and scope of activity. Perhaps, for Canada the challenge of the future might not be merely how to stimulate more great economic ventures that attest to Canadian power, but rather how to maximize the use of that power in a way that will develop individual Canadian talent and, at the same time, the individual talent of others striving for their own personal sense of identity.

Among the nations of the world Canada is a relatively new nation-state. Though constrained by biculturalism it has found some means for nationalistic expression without substantially impeding its economic growth. This is precisely the challenge facing the Commonwealth Caribbean. Yet, unlike Canada, the Commonwealth Caribbean lacks both the means and basic motivation for economic nationalism, for grand business ventures to be a release for the fervent nationalist. Such ventures have a way of invigorating a small population possessing an enormous land mass. The same cannot be said of the land-starved, population-glutted Commonwealth Caribbean. There a common rallying point for nationalism is race, and the cry becomes Black Nationalism.

It would be well if this work could end on a note of constructive suggestion and hope. It would be good if a positive program could be designed in which Canada, its banks, and the Commonwealth Caribbean could join. If the goal for Canada and its banks is the protection and enhancement of the Commonwealth Caribbean mini-states' individual sovereignty, it will be difficult indeed to suggest a program of cooperation, to offer hope. The brutal, objective reality is that many of the smaller nations simply do not have an economic potential on which to build. Left to their own individual resources, without tourism, in which the banks so often serve at least as advisors, some of the mini-states could not even provide for their population's marginal survival to say nothing of matching North American affluence. To a lesser extent the same can be said of the larger island states. There tourism is not as important as expertise in the wise use of resources.

The Canadian banks know and the Canadian government should know that the road to survival and growth in the Commonwealth Caribbean lies in regionalism. The Commonwealth Caribbean must be dealt with as an area if it is to develop fully. In a sense the Canadian government recognized this by the support it has given to the area's regional bank. But it may be another matter for the Canadian government to exercise policy initiatives that might induce still greater regionalism. To do so might interfere in other nations' sovereignty.

For Canada's banks the need for Canadian governmental support may be real. The banks and trust companies have entered fully into the employment of citizens in area where they do business. But, the next obvious step is to allow the transfer of employees between island-nations so that greater experience can be obtained. To do this, a freer work-permit policy must be instituted. The banks and trust companies have been substantially inhibited in bringing a higher level of training to Caribbean employees by the employment restrictions of the mini-states. The Canadian government apparently has not involved itself in the problem.

There are other examples that could be given. Capital movements between islands are severely limited. For a population of about four million there are now three central banks, and more on the way. With each central bank there is a separate currency. In such a climate how can growth take place?

For Canada to encourage regionalism and cooperate with its banks in bringing about such an end is, in a sense, asking Canada to engage in precisely the same kind of activity for which the Canadian economic nationalists condemned the United States government and its global corporations. Maybe the answer is in part that morality is not to be judged in terms of invading national sovereignty but, within reason, by each nation weighing its own economic interests and asking how it can assist the well-being of individuals. This is similar to asking the Canadian government to place itself in the shoes of its Commonwealth Caribbean banking enterprises and inquiring how they might serve the long-term needs of their customers. The position may prove uncomfortable to the Canadian government, but it should nevertheless be tried, for in a very real sense the Canadian banks are appendages of the Canadian government.

Whatever the Canadian government may attempt either alone or through its banks will not necessarily spell acceptance by the Commonwealth Caribbean. Nationalism can often be rooted in emotion which, in turn, can lead to self-destruction. The advice of outsiders can be cast aside, and for many purposes Canada and its banks are outsiders. Still, perhaps Canada in cooperation with its banks, a manifestation of Canadian nationalism, should make the effort to support the forces of regionalism even if it means a diminution of individual island sovereignty.

NOTES

1. Webster, "Low Key Protection of Canadian Independence and Not 'Massive Frontal Assault' Urged by PM," Toronto Globe and Mail, September 30, 1972, p. 10.

2. "International Trade," Progressive Conservative Headquarters Document No. 1320-59 (Ottawa, 1972), p. 4.

3. "Canadian Economic Independence," Progressive Conservative Headquarters Document No. 1320-57 (Ottawa, 1972), p. 2.

4. "Task Force on The Structure of Canadian Industry, Foreign Ownership and the Structure of Canadian Industry,"(Ottawa: Privy Council Office, 1968), pp. 2-3. Hereinafter cited as the Watkins Report.

5. Watkins Report, pp. 5-6.

6. Ibid., pp. 10-11.

7. Ibid., p. 17.

8. Ibid., pp. 19-20.

9. Ibid., pp. 360-361.

10. Ibid., p. 243.

11. Ibid., p. 96.

12. Ibid., p. 7.

13. A. Rotstein, "The Multi-National Corporation and The Nation-State," paper presented at the Annual Canadian-American Seminar, University of Windsor, November 21, 1968, p. 5. Professor Rotstein, of the Department of Political Economy, University of Toronto, was a member of the Watkins Task Force.

14. A. Safarian, Foreign Ownership of Canadian Industry (Toronto: McGraw-Hill, 1966), p. 311 (emphasis in original).

15. "A Citizen's Guide to the Herb Gray Report: Domestic Control of The National Economic Environment," The Canadian Forum, December 1971.

16. Foreign Direct Investment in Canada (Ottawa: Information Canada, 1972), p. v. Hereinafter cited as the Gray Report.

17 Ibid., pp. 479-480; see also pp. 456-461.

18. Ibid., p. 460.

19. Ibid., p. 462.

20. Ibid., p. 492.

21. Ibid., p. 438.

22. Gray Report, op. cit., p. 474.

23. "A Citizen's Guide to the Herb Gray Report," op. cit., p. 71.
24. Gray Report, op. cit., p. 392.
25. Isaiah Berlin, "The Bent Twig: A Note on Nationalism," Foreign Affairs 51 (October 1972): 24.
26. Ibid., p. 22.
27. Ibid., p. 23.
28. Ibid., p. 26.
29. Ibid., p. 28.
30. C. Hanly, "A Psychoanalysis of Nationalist Sentiment," Nationalism in Canada, P. Russell, ed. (Toronto, McGraw-Hill, 1966), pp. 303, 306-307.
31. F. Watt, "Nationalism in Canadian Literature," Nationalism in Canada, op. cit., pp. 235, 240.
32. Hanly, op. cit., p. 309.
33. See Canadian Annual Review for 1970, J. Saywell, ed. (Toronto: University of Toronto Press, 1971), pp. 346-355.
34. Hanly, op. cit., p. 312.
35. Ibid., p. 310.
36. C. Brown, "The Nationalism of The National Policy," Nationalism in Canada, op. cit., pp. 155, 162.
37. Hanly, op. cit., p. 318.

DANIEL JAY BAUM is Professor of Law and Administrative Studies at Osgoode Hall Law School, York University, Toronto, Canada. He is also a Regent of the Canadian Institute of Financial Planning.

Dr. Baum has extensive experience in matters relating to regulation of financial institutions and has served as a consultant to the Canadian Committee on Mutual Funds and Investment Contracts. His publications include The Investment Function of Canadian Financial Institutions (Praeger, 1973), and he is co-author with Ned Stiles of The Silent Partners: Institutional Investors and Corporate Control (Syracuse University Press, 1965). Dr. Baum is editor-in-chief of the Administrative Law Review, organ of the Administrative Law Section, American Bar Association.

Dr. Baum holds a B.A. and LL.B. from the University of Cincinnati and an LL.M. and J.S.D. from New York University.

DEVELOPMENT SAVINGS BANKS AND THE
THIRD WORLD: A Tool for the Diffusion of
Economic Power
> Chelliah Loganathan

INTERNATIONAL CONTROL OF FOREIGN
INVESTMENT: The Düsseldorf Conference on
Multinational Corporations
> edited by Don Wallace, Jr. assisted by
> Helga Ruof-Koch

THE INVESTMENT FUNCTION OF CANADIAN
FINANCIAL INSTITUTIONS
> Daniel J. Baum

THE MULTINATIONAL CORPORATION AS A
FORCE IN LATIN AMERICAN POLITICS:
A Case Study of the International Petroleum
Company in Peru
> Adalberto J. Pinelo

MULTINATIONAL CORPORATIONS IN WORLD
DEVELOPMENT
> United Nations Department of Eco-
> nomic and Social Affairs

THE POLITICAL RISKS FOR MULTINATIONAL
ENTERPRISE IN DEVELOPING COUNTRIES:
With a Case Study of Peru
> Dolph Warren Zink

978-0-595-47603-9
0-595-47603-1

www.ingramcontent.com/pod-product-compliance
Lightning Source LLC
Chambersburg PA
CBHW031052180526
45163CB00002BA/797